Just Enough Database

1st Edition

Just Enough Database

Design, Querying, and Programming.

An Introduction to interacting with a database as a software developer.

Part of the "Just Enough" series on the practices and techniques of software development.

Ed Crookshanks
Nokel Services
Summer 2017

Cover image: Kelsey Crookshanks

ISBN-13: 978-1973921691
ISBN-10: 1973921693

Version 2017-Summer

To Amy, Noah, and Kelsey

TABLE OF CONTENTS

Preface

About the "Just Enough" Series
This series of books is aimed at programmers who are new to formal development, or those seasoned programmers who would like to gain an understanding of processes they haven't used or been exposed to. Common examples would be recent graduates or those taking some type of "Software Practicum" course; someone who is self-taught or a hobbyist and is looking to move to the corporate world; or someone who has worked in very small software organizations where development is less controlled. Although there may be statements about retail software the emphasis is mainly on enterprise software within a medium to large organization.

Each book provides a relatively brief but in-depth discussion of its topic. While I dare not say that each book "is really all you need to know" on a particular topic, I feel that the major points and most frequently used practices and techniques are discussed. There are thousands of software producing organizations out there and there is no way to even come close to discussing the fine points that each organization uses. However there are some common practices and techniques that are the same or similar in principle. My aim is to keep these topics relatively short and more at a "getting started" level than a "deep dive" into each. As someone who has interviewed many people I can attest to the fact that hearing "I'm familiar with the concept and I've worked through some examples" is much better than "I've never heard of or used that technique." At the very least during interviews I hope to enable the first answer with books in this series.

Another reason that I'm not going into extreme detail on each topic is that there are many other books with hundreds of pages that do that. I would rather introduce these topics to a level that is quickly usable, thereby letting the reader decide which to investigate further based on experience or interest. Learning, especially in IT/programming, is a life-long pursuit and while techniques usually change slower than technology both do evolve at a pace that is quicker than other engineering disciplines.

With that, I hope to keep each book in this series at under one hundred pages and group the topics so that they flow together and are complementary. Brevity will be key in that; examples will be kept simple and code will often be "snipped" to exclude items not directly being discussed.

Notes about Software

Examples are provided mostly in C# and Microsoft tools, all of which have some level of free software available, such as Visual Studio Community Edition. Enterprise versions of these tools may exist, or similar tools with stricter licensing models and slightly different semantics may exist; it is simply assumed that tools at the educational level will be closer to the free versions. Also, most hobby developers or recent graduates will probably make use of free tools instead of starting with an expensive development tool suite. If a particular topic/example is not given in a familiar language or with a familiar tool it should be easily translated into another environment. Where possible, notes on how different platforms solve different problems in different ways will be noted. Some of these tools may already be mandated by an employer, others may be free to choose which tools to use to start a practice discussed here.

Please note – the examples will be kept necessarily simple. In fact, most of the examples will be so short that the tools and techniques used on them will probably not seem worth it. However in the context of much larger systems, enterprise systems, these tools and techniques are very useful.

Author Summary

Ed Crookshanks has over 20 years of experience in software development. He started with C on a VAX machine for medical research, moved on to C++ on both Unix and PC platforms, database programming, and finally added some Java and .NET in a wide variety of business domains. He is also a former adjunct professor and a Microsoft Certified Trainer delivering classes on SQL Server and Visual Studio. A full bio can be found at http://www.nokelservices.com/bio.html.

Introduction

Just about every software application stores data in some form or fashion. Although there is a recent push to non-relational storage, table-based relational database structures are by far the most prevalent storage mechanism in use today. Especially in larger organizations where a solid infrastructure exists as well as corporate or regulatory mandates concerning aspects such as auditing, redundancy, security, etc. Structured Query Language (SQL) is even supported in many non-relational storage frameworks.

In this book I will introduce the reader to relational theory and database design, the SQL language and its use, language libraries and Object-Relational Mapping (ORM) tools, and how all of this fits together in a typical application. The database tools used will be Microsoft SQL Server ® and supporting libraries and frameworks. These are freely downloadable from Microsoft.

The SQL language is standardized, but each database platform (Microsoft, Oracle, MySQL, etc.) typically has "extensions" to the language that enhance one or more areas of functionality. There are also minor differences in terminology and syntax; the aim in this book will be to use common terms and syntax and point out any significant differences to any other database platforms. However it should also be trivial to transfer most theory, statements, and programming constructs to other platforms and SQL language implementations.

While much database design and implementation can be done with graphical tools this book will use SQL statements as the basis for all implementation. The reasoning behind this is two-fold. First, graphical tools usually end up generating the type of statements that will be used here whether the user sees them or not. Knowing the theory behind the tools can often result in better design or at least less headache. Secondly, in an environment with separation of duties, the database administrator who creates the structures will want or need these statements. Or if the creation of the database or modifications is automated, scripted statements are absolutely necessary in this scenario.

Database Design

There are two main types of relational databases – normalized, which are designed for frequent input and constant change, and dimensional, which is best suited for reporting and data warehousing. Data warehousing is out of scope for this book; I will be focused entirely on the normalized database model.

First, some very basic definitions. A database is mainly comprised of tables which can be thought of as the nouns of design. Person, car, building, etc. are often modeled as tables in a database. Tables are composed of attributes such as height, weight, eye color, phone number, etc. The entire combination is frequently referred to in terms similar to a spreadsheet – individual objects are the "rows" of the table and each attribute is in its own "column". A "key" is an identifier for a row. Other components of a database will be defined later as I introduce other constructs.

With the definitions out of the way, what does "normal" refer to? For a database the term "normal" refers to the structure of the data; "normalized" refers to the degree to which the data adheres to the "normal forms" - the rules of normalization. These forms and the accompanying theory are detailed in (Codd, 2000); the following paragraphs are a summary of those theories and rules with additional practical discussion.

There are three normal forms, each of which build on the previous. So Second Normal Form (2NF) indicates First Normal Form (1NF) has already been satisfied, and Third Normal Form (3NF) implies 1NF and 2NF are satisfied also.

Note that in theory these are rigid rules; in practice there are sometimes performance or usability reasons to "bend the rules". Terms such as "highly normalized" or "loosely Third Normal" may be seen and imply strict or less strict adherence to the rules.

Natural vs. Surrogate Primary Keys

Before we talk about the normal forms it is important to discuss the concept of a "key". The value or values that designate each row unique is known as the "key" and is made of one or more columns. The key can either part of the data itself (known as natural) or an arbitrarily assigned value (known as a surrogate). There are some lively arguments over natural versus surrogate keys; the definition of each will be given below and I will try to stay out of the overt promotion of either one.

A natural key is one or more particular columns that would uniquely identify each row. A typical example would be a person table with a Social Security Number as a natural key. Or a car table with a VIN column as the key. Purely by nature of the data these values are guaranteed to be unique for each entry. A multiple column example could be a magazine table, with Title and Publishing Date as a composite (multi-column) key. These values are all valid attributes of the object and they uniquely identify each row of data. Database engines have constraint properties that enforce the uniqueness among the value of the column (or columns) and won't let duplicates be added.

Surrogate primary keys are values, often simply integers, which uniquely identify each row. Some refer to this as "row id" and it is simply called "ID" or "TableNameID" where TableName is the name of the table. The controversy arises in that this value has absolutely no relation to the data; its sole purpose is to enforce row uniqueness.

During the upcoming discussion the term key will be used as a generic term for a unique identifier and natural or surrogate will not be differentiated. Another type of key is a "foreign key" – this is a value in one table that identifies a row in another table. This is how relations are determined and will be discussed further a little later when multiple tables are discussed.

First Normal Form (1NF)

First Normal Form states that each table represents a single entity, there are no collections of data in a single column, and each row is unique. Essentially this means each row represents only one entity and each column has only a single value. An example of a table that does not meet these rules is an Employee table shown below in Figure 1.

The table in Figure 1 violates 1NF because the Work Location column has a comma separated list of values for DaBoss. In addition to violating 1NF this type of column data would increase the work required on any application that consumed this data.

EmployNum	FirstName	LastName	Work Location
22	Ted	Johnson	Room 1
33	Joann	Wexley	Room 2
44	Alice	Wonderland	Room 3
55	Tom	DaBoss	Room 4, Room 5

Figure 1 - Violating 1NF

Every time a Work Location value was read it would have to be checked and/or parsed for multiple values. Figure 2 shows another example of how 1NF could be violated. For space Work Location has been abbreviated, but the idea of multiple columns has the same violations and challenges as multiple values in one column.

EmployNum	FirstName	LastName	Loc 1	Loc 2
22	Ted	Johnson	Room 1	
33	Joann	Wexley	Room 2	
44	Alice	Wonderland	Room 3	
55	Tom	DaBoss	Room 4	Room 5

Figure 2 - 1NF Violation

Figure 3 shows a table that satisfies the original technical definition of 1NF. It also highlights a common issue with only having 1NF data – partial duplication.

EmployNum	FirstName	LastName	Work Location
22	Ted	Johnson	Room 1
33	Joann	Wexley	Room 2
44	Alice	Wonderland	Room 3
55	Tom	DaBoss	Room 4
55	Tom	DaBoss	Room 5

Figure 3 - 1NF Table.

Even though the data meets 1NF requirements, the duplication of the three pieces of information is not pleasant. Processing the data on a record-by-record basis would be confusing. That duplication is solved by further normalizing the data.

Second Normal Form (2NF)

Only tables that are in 1NF can be further refined into 2NF, which states that in addition to 1NF all the table's non-key columns must be dependent on *ONLY* the key column or columns and must be dependent on the entire key, not part of it. This promotes and further regulates the intention of a table representing one and only one idea. This also starts a sometimes subjective debate on relational attributes and keys.

The table discussed so far is the Employee table, so to be in 2NF all columns not part of the key must be dependent on only the key. Initially looking at Figure 3 one would deduce that the EmployNum and Work Location columns could be combined for a key and therefore each record is unique.

However the problem is that the FirstName and LastName columns only depend on the EmployNum column. The term "depends on" can be thought of as meaning a one-way relationship in both directions. So EmployNum 55 always results in LastName "DaBoss", and "DaBoss" always results in EmployNum 55. This can't be said for Work Location therefore LastName/FirstName is dependent on only part of the identified key.

Another problem arises in that Work Location isn't really an intrinsic property of an employee. From a data modeling perspective (or even an object-oriented design perspective) a Work Location is really a separate entity. So if we think from the perspective the EmployNum should be the sole identifier of an employee and the Work Location isn't dependent on that value (since it is different for the same key). So to fully comply with good design principles and be in 2NF Work Location should be removed.

So then how is it accessed and associated with an employee? A Work Location table is created and a construct known as a "foreign key" relates the two entities. Each of these tables are in 2NF and they are related by a column in the Work Location table that identifies.

Figure 4 shows the revised Employee table while Figure 5 shows the newly created Work Location table; each is in 2NF. While it may not look like the Work Location table is in 2NF because of the repeated EmployNum value, that column is a "foreign key" column and doesn't count as a table attribute in the consideration of forms. Work Location also makes use of a surrogate key, Location ID. This really isn't necessary in this simple example but is used only for illustrative purposes.

EmployNum	FirstName	LastName
22	Ted	Johnson
33	Joann	Wexley
44	Alice	Wonderland
55	Tom	DaBoss

Figure 4 - Employee Table

Location ID	Work Location	EmployNum
1	Room 1	22
2	Room 2	33
3	Room 3	44
4	Room 4	55
5	Room 5	55

Figure 5 - Work Location Table

Third Normal Form (3NF)

For a table to be in 3NF it must be in 2NF and all the non-key columns must be dependent ONLY on the primary key. In more simple terms this means that non-key columns cannot be dependent on or derived from other non-key columns.

One very simple example of this in the design so far would be the inclusion of a "Number Of Rooms" column in the Employee table. Figure 6 shows this violation. Not only is the Number of Rooms value not dependent on the key, this is a value that can be derived by other means as well (as will be shown later in querying examples).

EmployNum	FirstName	LastName	NumberOfRooms
22	Ted	Johnson	1
33	Joann	Wexley	1
44	Alice	Wonderland	1
55	Tom	DaBoss	2

Figure 6 - Violation of 3NF

Quick/Lazy Definition of Normal Form

While the previous definitions of Normal Form are steeped in theory there is often practically acceptable criteria that renders a database "normal enough."

- Each table represents a single entity.
- Each row is identified by a primary key.
- All non-key columns are single values and are dependent on or derived from only the primary key.
- Foreign keys are used as relational attributes between related entities.
- Columns that violate 3NF must be kept to an absolute minimum and must represent a significant performance saving to justify.

This last "exception rule" can be loosely interpreted as follows. If a summary value such as Number of Rooms can be calculated with a simple query then it should be calculated by a query. If however the summary value can only be calculated by a much more complicated query, such as combining multiple tables, using special functions, etc., then the storage cost of the additional data should be weighed against the complexity and performance of the calculation. This can be a very subjective answer and so practicality versus theory can sometimes be a lively discussion.

One to One, Many to One, and Many to Many

The relationship in Figure 4 and Figure 5 between Work Location and Employee is known as a "many to one" relationship because the table with the foreign key, Work Location, can have many different entries that map to a single entity in the primary key table, Employee. Multiple locations are related to a single employee. Depending on the perspective this can also be referred to as a "one to many" and I will use the terms interchangeably throughout the book.

In sentence form, it is said that "an employee can have multiple rooms, but a room can only belong to one employee." This type of verbal analysis is an important tool in design as it can determine the type of relationship.

Another type of relationship is One to One. This occurs when two tables are related as before with a foreign key, but the foreign key is only allowed to refer to a single entity in the other table. An example of this, an employee as a manager of a department, will be shown later when the full database is discussed.

The most complex relation is a Many to Many relationship. This occurs when both entities can have multiple related entities in the other table. An example of this would an Employee-Project relationship if employees are allowed participate in multiple projects. In sentence form "an employee can have multiple projects, and a project can have multiple employees."

Since both entity tables have a primary key that identifies unique rows it is not possible to identify multiple related rows in either of the original entity tables. A third table is used that holds both entity keys in a single row and has a composite key consisting of both entries. This third table is often called a join table, bridge table, or junction table.

Figures 7 and 8 show the additional tables for this type of relationship. Each row in the join table consists of an EmployeeNum and a ProjectID which uniquely identifies that combination. No other information is needed in the join table as all other information is contained in the related tables.

ProjectID	Name	StartDate	PctComplete
1	Proj 1	4/1/2017	20
2	Proj 2	3/12/2017	30
3	Proj 3	3/19/2017	25
4	Proj 4	7/1/2017	0

Figure 7 - Project Table

EmployNum	ProjID
22	1
33	1
44	2
33	2
22	3
44	1

Figure 8 - Employee-Project Join Table

In a complex database there could be multiple relationships in a single table. An Employee could have the additional relationships from a department, building, or other tables. And one table could have multiple foreign keys in it, meaning it has relationships to many different tables. This is shown and discussed below in the ER diagram.

ER Diagram

The ER (Entity Relationship) Diagram is a common data modeling technique for describing overall database structure. There are common notations and representations that allow viewers of the diagram to deduce the relationships and rules of the database.

Many tools exist for creating an ER diagram. Some database tools will generate a diagram based on an existing database. Other tools allow the user to create the database in a visual manner by dragging and dropping shapes and connecting entities. Some allow for taking the model and generating database creation statements from the model. This allows users to create a database from design to physical creation without writing SQL.

Figure 9 shows a basic model for the Employee database taken directly from Microsoft SQL Server Management Studio. Other tools may have slightly different symbols, but the underlying concepts are the same. In the diagram, key symbol beside a column represents the primary key of the table. Between related tables the end of the line with a key is "one" side of the relationship, and the infinity symbol represents the "many" side of the relationship. When reading from one table to another the proper interpretation is on the "to" side. For example, Employee "TO" WorkLocation – the many symbol is next to the "TO" table, so an Employee can have many Locations. Reading from the other direction a WorkLocation can only point to one Employee because the key symbol is on the "TO" side of the relation reading that way.

A few of the relationships need more explanation. The first is between Employee and Department. Notice that there are actually two relationships, both a many to one and a one to one. The many to one is so that many Employees can belong to one Department and uses the DeptID column in both tables.

The other relationship between Employee and Department is a one to one, notated by a key being on each end. This is between the EmloyeeNum and ManagerID columns. How is this done so that the system recognizes it as one to one and not one to many?

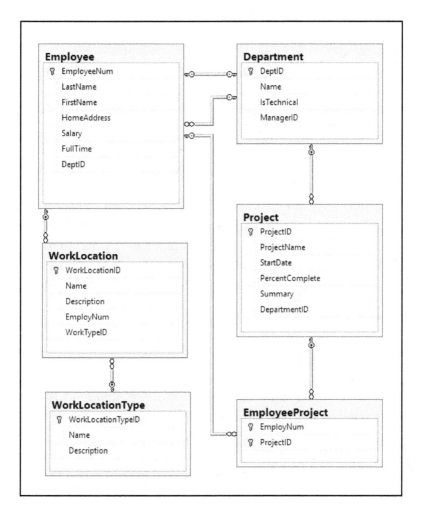

Figure 9 - Employee Database ER Diagram

To enforce the one to one, a normal Foreign Key relationship is setup between ManagerID (as the FK) and EmployeeNum. Notice the names of the columns are not required to be the same, only the data types. Once this is set up a "Unique Constraint" (discussed later) is set up on the ManagerID column in Department. This constraint enforces a restriction of the column containing no duplicate values. Hence since the Primary Key on Employee is guaranteed to be unique, and the ManagerID in Department is also guaranteed to be unique, that creates a one to one relationship between the two tables for Department Manager.

Finally, the visual representation of the many to many is shown with the EmployeeProject table. It has two relationships defined – a one to many from the Project table, and a one to many from the Employee table. As discussed before this allows for Employees to work on many Projects and Projects to have many people. Later on it will be shown how this join table works and how it complicates the queries.

Other Constructs

In addition to the data modeling techniques that have been discussed so far, there are some additional database constructs that are important to have a passing knowledge of as a programmer. The next few paragraphs will discuss these at a fairly high level; in-depth discussion can be found in platform specific references or more in-depth database administrator resources.

Constraints were mentioned previously in the one to one example. In that case a UNIQUE constraint was applied to a column - the database engine then enforces the rule that all values in the column are unique across all rows, disallowing any repeated values.

A CHECK constraint is another very common constraint applied to a database column. This is essentially a Boolean expression that the database engine enforces when inserting or updating data. Without getting into SQL syntax, an example would be "PercentComplete > 0" to disallow negative numbers in that column. Another may be "FullTime IN ('Y', 'N')" to ensure that the FullTime value is either 'Y' or 'N'. These constraints can also reference other columns, so if the Project table later had an "EndDate" column added, a good CHECK constraint for that column would be "EndDate > StartDate" to enforce the rule that the end was always after the beginning.

Other specifiers can act like constraints but not be declared in the same way. Often there is a specifier for "NOT NULL" which means that the column must be provided a value. In conjunction with that there is sometimes a DEFAULT specifier such that if a value isn't provided the DEFAULT is used.

One other common term that needs discussing is an INDEX. An INDEX is a database construct that is meant to increase performance of looking up values. So far we've discussed the PRIMARY KEY and this is actually a type of INDEX. The database will often order the table by this key; therefore if searching for a particular record via its index the database can used special search algorithms to locate the row. Contrast this with the other option – searching each individual row until the value is found.

Secondary INDEXes can also be created on a table, often times on the foreign key columns. This speeds up searching between tables. Although the table can't be ordered by these secondary INDEXes, the database often creates a secondary list somewhere as a separate entity. This list can be searched in an efficient manner and the resulting full record retrieved after the correct value is located. Again this is more efficient than searching the entire table in sequential order.

Finally, before diving into queries it is important to know a little about datatypes. The diagram in Figure 9 had no types, but a more complete table listing is shown in Figure 10. A complete discussion of all the datatypes are beyond the scope of this book and can better be found in platform specific documentation. There are standard types, extended types, synonyms for types, etc. that are more completely described elsewhere.

The `int` data type is for standard numeric integers; there are also `float` and `decimal` datatypes for non-integer values. Also, `money` is a specific type that is a custom decimal for monetary values. The `bit` type can have 1 or 0, typically to represent true or false.

The one type that is essential to understand is the VARCHAR datatype. VARCHAR is short for VARiable CHARacter and describes a string that can be up to the specified length. Thus VARCHAR(30) can be up to 30 characters in length. "Up to" is the key phrase, the database will only use as much storage as is needed which can be a significant space savings in certain situations. A string specified as CHAR(30) would always take up 30 bytes in each row which could potentially waste a lot of space.

Sometimes the type NVARCHAR is used. This is the double-byte equivalent which can be used for extended character sets. However the same rule applies – only the number of spaces required to hold the value are used and nothing more.

Employee

Column Name	Data Type	Allow Nulls
♀ EmployeeNum	int	☐
LastName	varchar(50)	☐
FirstName	varchar(30)	☐
HomeAddress	varchar(50)	☐
Salary	money	☐
FullTime	bit	☐
DeptID	int	☑
		☐

Figure 10 - Table and Data Types

Notice the "Allow Nulls" value is also visible. As noted above this is for specifying if a value is required for a particular column. In the table above only the "DeptID" column is allowed to be blank. From are previous discussion on foreign keys this means that an Employee isn't required to be part of a Department. However if they are the foreign key constraint will ensure that the value for DeptID exists in the Department table.

Writing Queries

Before jumping in and writing query statements, it is important to learn that there are actually multiple types of queries. All are SQL statements but they are often classified in three broad classes. Data Control Language (DCL) statements are SQL statements that control object permissions in the database. Creating users and giving the read or read/write access to a table is an example of this type of statement. As this is the realm of the Database Administrator (DBA) those statements won't be discussed here.

Data Definition Language (DDL) statements are how the actual tables and other structures are created. While many tools allow for graphical creation knowing how to script objects is also valuable. Many times a DBA will only accept SQL statements as a means to perform database creation and/or manipulation.

```
CREATE TABLE Employee(
       EmployeeNum int NOT NULL,
       LastName varchar(50) NOT NULL,
       FirstName varchar(30) NOT NULL,
       HomeAddress varchar(50) NOT NULL,
       Salary money NOT NULL,
       FullTime bit NOT NULL,
       DeptID int NULL,
  CONSTRAINT PK_Employee
       PRIMARY KEY CLUSTERED (EmployeeNum ASC)  )
```

Figure 11 - Table Creation Statement

Figure 11 is the simplified SQL statement for creating the Employee table in the example database. Notice how each column is specified as Name, Type, and Null Specifier. Also note that the primary key is named (PK_Employee) and specified as a CONSTRAINT on the EmployeeNum column. This reinforces the earlier discussion of the not only understanding the logical concept of a key, but also the physical implementation of it as a constraint. There are similar CREATE statements for the entire database as well as most other database objects.

One note about the Employee table. The EmployeeNum primary key is a natural key and the value comes from the data. Many other tables in the database use surrogate keys. Those table CREATE statements look like Figure 12.

```
CREATE TABLE Project (
      ProjectID int IDENTITY(1,1) NOT NULL,
      ProjectName varchar(30) NOT NULL,
      StartDate date NOT NULL,
      PercentComplete int NOT NULL,
      Summary varchar(200) NULL,
      DepartmentID int NULL,
  CONSTRAINT PK_Project
      PRIMARY KEY CLUSTERED (ProjectID ASC) )
```

Figure 12 - CREATE with Identity column

Very similar to Figure 11, but the addition of the IDENTITY(1,1) clause has a special meaning. Rather than a user-defined primary key IDENTITY signifies that the database will assign unique values (starting at 1, incrementing by 1) for the column. Unlike natural keys these shouldn't be provided when creating the data.

Data Manipulation Language (DML) statements are the largest and most common group and are the primary means of manipulating data. The rest of this section and the majority of the remainder of the book will discuss these statements.

Although the SELECT statement is by far the most used SQL statement, I will start with a basic INSERT statement. To get data into the database many INSERT statements similar to Figure 13 are used.

```
INSERT INTO Employee (EmployeeNum, LastName,
FirstName, HomeAddress, Salary, FullTime)
VALUES (22, 'Johnson', 'Ted', '123 Ted Street',
       100000.00, 1)
```

Figure 13 - Simple INSERT (Natural key)

Again, owing to the difference in primary key types, the Project table (and other surrogate key tables) are populated with statements similar to Figure 14. The primary key column is not included and its value is provided by the database.

```
INSERT INTO Project (ProjectName, StartDate,
                PercentComplete, Summary)
VALUES('Xamarin Mobile App', '3-JUL-2017',
        0, 'Simple Xamarin POC for HR')
```

Figure 14 - Simple INSERT (Identity column)

The full script for creating and populating the database is in the appendix.

Retrieving Data

The SELECT statement is used to retrieve data. It is by far the most common SQL statement and arguably the most complex as well. However its basic form is alarmingly simple as shown in Figure 15.

```
SELECT column_list
FROM
table_name
```

Figure 15 - Basic SELECT Syntax

> NOTE:
> In all the following SQL code, SQL Language statements will be capitalized and placeholders will be in lowercase italics to denote the different parts of the statement. Actual database objects will be Capitalized non-italics.

The `column_list` is a list of desired columns, and `table_name` is the actual name of the table. Based on the Employee table in the database are several forms of this basic query. A very common shortcut is shown below:

```
SELECT *
FROM
Employee
```

Figure 16 - Basic SELECT (Bad form)

The "*" is a shortcut for "all columns". It is often used for quick manual research queries, but is largely considered bad form. The reason is two-fold. One is that it will often bring back way more information than is needed. Even for a small table such as our Employee table, the result set was too wide to fit in the width of this single page. The second reason is in prepared statements, such as stored procedures or other programming constructs (explained later), the query would produce different results if the table changed. Programming and remote database connections also have a factor of too much information; for performance reasons only the data that is of interest should be returned.

Explicitly named columns provide a way to retrieve only the data of interest. The query and the result set are shown next.

```
SELECT LastName, FirstName, HomeAddress
FROM Employee
```

LastName	FirstName	HomeAddress
Johnson	Ted	123 Ted Street
Wexley	Joann	454 CID Place
Wonderland	Alice	The Yellowbrick Road
Daboss	Tom	1 King Street
Moore	Gary	6 String Blvd
Sister	Twisted	Take It Lane
Wilde	Zack	88 Big Band Street

Figure 17 - Select Columns and Result Set

Notice how only the columns requested are displayed. Also notice that the column names in the result set are the same names as the database column names. This is not always desirable both for readability and ambiguity. To get around this there is a common practice known as 'aliasing' names which SQL allows.

```
SELECT E.LastName AS "Last Name"
, E.FirstName AS [First Name]
, E.HomeAddress AS [Home Address]
FROM Employee E
```

Last Name	First Name	Street Address
Johnson	Ted	123 Ted Street
Wexley	Joann	454 CID Place
Wonderland	Alice	The Yellowbrick Road
Daboss	Tom	1 King Street
Moore	Gary	6 String Blvd
Sister	Twisted	Take It Lane
Wilde	Zack	88 Big Band Street

Figure 18 - SELECT with Aliases

Both quotes ("") and brackets ([]) were used in the above example because the aliases contain spaces. Any time an identifier contains spaces or is a reserved word it must be delimited with double quotes. Brackets are a SQL Server alternative and are used extensively in Microsoft code and generated statements. The statements in this book may use either syntax, just keep in mind that double quotes are the ANSI standard and statements written with them should translate to other databases.

The keyword "AS" is used in Figure 18 as well, but it should be noted that it is optional. The statement uses "AS" explicitly to rename each column but omits it when aliasing the Employee table as "E". Table aliasing is overkill in this example but will become important in the next section when a table is reference multiple times or multiple tables are used in a single query.

As powerful as the simple SELECT statement is, it is very limited in its usability. When thousands or even millions of records are present in a table a way of narrowing down the amount of data retrieved is needed. Figure 19 shows the syntax for a SQL SELECT statement with additional qualifiers for filtering and sorting data.

```
SELECT column_list
FROM table_name
WHERE predicate
ORDER BY column_name [ASC/DESC]
```

Figure 19 - Filter and Order syntax

NOTE:
Many of the following example will use "*" for brevity and not include the actual result set, but simply a description of how the results would be presented. The result set will only be shown if needed to supplement the description.

First will be examples of the `WHERE` clause. The *predicate* is a Boolean expression that involves operators and columns. There can be one expression or several joined together.

The expressions can be standard numerical operators (<, >, >=, <=, etc.), set operators, string operators, or built-in function operators. The following grid shows several of these with explanations of each. In any case the database engine uses the expressions to decide which rows to include in the result set.

`SELECT E.LastName FROM Employee E WHERE E.Salary > 100000`	Last name of Employees with a salary greater than 100,000.
`SELECT * FROM Employee E WHERE E.EmployeeNum = 33`	Only EmployeeNum 33.
`SELECT * FROM Employee E WHERE E.EmployeeNum IN (33, 44, 55)`	Employees with EmployeeNum of 33, 44, or 55.
`SELECT * FROM Employee E WHERE E.Salary BETWEEN 90000 AND 120000`	Employees with Salaries greater than/equal to 90000 and less than/equal to 120000.
`SELECT * FROM Employee E WHERE E.Salary >= 120000 AND E.FullTime = 1`	All full time employees with a salary greater than or equal to 120000.
`SELECT * FROM Employee E WHERE E.DeptiID IS NULL`	Employees with no relationship to Department.

Figure 20 - Sample WHERE clauses

Although most statements in Figure 20 are explained well enough by the description column there are a few additional nuances that need explained. The first query illustrates that a column in the `WHERE` clause doesn't need to be in the `SELECT` clause. Also note the syntax of the `IN` and `BETWEEN` statements – one uses parenthesis and the other does not. In the fifth query different columns may be in different clauses and a logical operator combines the results.

Lastly, the `IS NULL` clause shows the special way in which `NULL` is treated. Technically the NULL value is undefined, so a comparison using = doesn't really work because two undefined cant truly be compared. `IS NULL` and its companion negative form `IS NOT NULL` are the preferred way to check columns for NULL values.

Strings have a different syntax for finding and comparing values. The use of "=" is straight forward, except for something known as Collation. Collation is how the database engine stores, interprets, and compares character data. It can be set for different languages and orderings, but in general the most important option is for case-sensitive or case-insensitive string comparison. Depending on how that is set 'TED' = 'Ted' can either be true or false.

The set of queries in Figure 21 demonstrate typical string `WHERE` condition operations. Note that to guard against case sensitivity the second query uses a built-in function for transforming the column value before comparison.

`SELECT * FROM Employee E` `WHERE E.FirstName = 'Ted'`	Last name of Employees with a FirstName equal to 'Ted'. (See notes above)

`SELECT * FROM Employee E`
`WHERE`
`UPPER(E.FirstName) = 'TED'`
	Using the UPPER function and an uppercase string to guard again case sensitivity.

`SELECT * FROM Employee E`
`WHERE`
`LOWER(E.FirstName) = 'ted'`
	Same as the previous query except using the alternative case comparison.

`SELECT * FROM Employee E`
`WHERE UPPER(E.FirstName)`
`IN ('TED', 'TOM')`
	All employees with FirstName of Ted or Tom.

`SELECT * FROM Employee E` `WHERE E.FirstName LIKE 'T%'`	All employees with FirstName begin with T with any number of letters next. (% is the SQL wildcard)

`SELECT * FROM Employee E`
`WHERE E.FirstName`
`LIKE 'T_m%'`
	All employees with FirstName begin with T, have any letter next, then an m, then any letters following. (i.e. Tommy, Tammy, Tamara, etc.)

`SELECT * FROM Employee E`
`WHERE FirstName LIKE 'Tam%'`
`AND LastName LIKE '%s%'`
	Employees with a FirstName starting with 'Tam' and LastName with an 's' in it.

Figure 21 - String WHERE clauses

The previous examples are straight forward, with the exception of the last query. It's easy to understand but a little more difficult to understand why it is bad. It has to do with the way the database engine processes the wildcard character and performance.

For the clause `LIKE 'Tam%'` the database can perform that filter quickly because it can easily skip rows that don't have a FirstName starting with Tam. However for the second clause, `LIKE '%s%'`, there is now way to narrow that down without examining every row's LastName column since the wildcard is both before and after the letter of interest.

There are several other string functions that are often useful when comparing strings. Some common ones are listed and described below in Figure 22.

String functions are one area where there may be significant difference among different platforms. For example the SQL Server `LEN()` function below is called `LENGTH()` in other databases. While there is a SQL Standard function named `CONCAT()` to combine two strings, SQL Server uses a standard "+" symbol.

Another greatly variable region is time and date types and comparisons. The database documentation is the best place to look for that so it will be very briefly touched on here as there is only one table with Date information. In the Project table there is a `StartDate` column of type `Date`. There is also a `DateTime` type which would include time information but that isn't used here.

`TRIM(string)`	Remove spaces from both ends of the string.
`RTRIM(string)` `LTRIM(string)`	Trims all blank spaces from the right or left of a string.
`CHARINDEX(string1, string2)`	Returns the integer index of where string2 begins inside of string1, or -1 if not found.
`SUBSTRING(string, start, Length)`	Pulls out the characters starting at *start* and going for *length* characters.
`LEN(string)`	Returns the length of the string.

Figure 22 - Additional String Functions

In SQL Server it is OK to compare a date to a string, as in `StartDate > '14-May-2016'`, but there are a few caveats. One is that the string has to be in a format that can be recognized as a date. The previous example is a very common one, as is `'5-14-2017'` and `'5/14/2017'`. This can also be collation/location sensitive as some cultures put the day first, as in `'14-5-2017'`. If however no delimiters are used then the year must come first – `'20170514'`.

Another is that if a Date or a DateTime are used and no time information is given, the assumption is midnight – 00:00:00. This can be important when searching for ranges when times are involved. If a user wanted to find projects started on the 14th and 15th a WHERE clause such as StartDate >= '14-May-2016' and StartDate <= '15-May-2016' might be used. However, this will only include projects for the 14th and none for the 15th (unless a Date type is used or the time is specifically entered as 00:00:00). This is because if any entries for the 15th include a time later than midnight it will not be picked up by the <= operator.

ORDER BY is a simple comma separated list of columns to sort the results. The optional ASC and DESC are for specifying ascending or descending order, respectively. If not specified ascending is the default order.

So far there has only been one table involved in the queries. While this is good for demonstration purposes, practical queries often involve more than one table. Earlier in discussing keys the concept of a foreign key was discussed to relate two tables together. The next set of queries demonstrate how that is used.

```
SELECT column_list
FROM table_one t1
[INNER | [LEFT|RIGHT OUTER] | FULL]
JOIN
Table_two t2
ON t1.foreign_key = t2.primary_key
```

Figure 23 - Simple JOIN Syntax

The syntax [INNER | OUTER | FULL] means that
those keywords are optional. After explaining a very basic
example next those keywords will be added and explained.
Also, aliases are shown in the syntax but not technically
required. If not used the full table name would be used.

```
SELECT E.FirstName, E.LastName,
D.Name AS "Dept Name"
FROM Employee E
JOIN
Department D
ON E.DeptID = D.DeptID
```

Figure 24 - Simple JOIN query

The query in Figure 24 combines the rows from the
Employee and Department tables based on matching
DeptID values. These tables are shown in Figure 25. The
value of aliases is evident here as it is much easier to type
"E" and "D" rather than the full table names. The result set,
shown in Figure 26, contains the values from three columns
of the combined tables and also uses aliases
advantageously. Notice the result set can include columns
from either table as long as they are properly identified.
Strictly speaking the alias isn't needed in the above query
because each column name is unique between the
combined tables. for instance, if there were more than one
"Name" column in the combined tables it would be required
to identify which one to display by including the table name
or alias. The above query uses aliases for readability and
clarity of where the value is coming from.

Since there is no modifier for the JOIN clause, the default is an INNER JOIN and the query could be written as such with the exact same results. This type of join is also sometimes referred to as an EQUI-JOIN because only rows that have matches are included. That is, only rows in the Employee and Department tables that have matching DeptID values are included.

EmployeeNum	LastName	FirstName	DeptID
22	Johnson	Ted	19
33	Wexley	Joann	19
44	Wonderland	Alice	1
55	Daboss	Tom	20
66	Moore	Gary	21
77	Sister	Twisted	22
88	Wilde	Zack	NULL

DeptID	Name
1	External Programming
19	Internal Programming
20	Marketing
21	HR
22	Infrastructure

Figure 25 - Tables to be joined

FirstName	LastName	Dept Name
Ted	Johnson	Internal Programming
Joann	Wexley	Internal Programming
Alice	Wonderland	External Programming
Tom	Daboss	Marketing
Gary	Moore	HR
Twisted	Sister	Infrastructure

Figure 26 - Sample query result set

OUTER JOIN statements are different. They include rows in the result set that have no match and represented by NULL entries. The specifier LEFT or RIGHT is required (actually the word OUTER is optional; a LEFT JOIN or RIGHT JOIN statement is always OUTER) and indicates from which table to include non-matching rows. Figure 27 below shows the statement written as a LEFT OUTER JOIN and the result set produced.

```
SELECT E.FirstName, E.LastName,
D.Name AS "Dept Name"
FROM Employee E
LEFT OUTER JOIN
Department D
ON E.DeptID = D.DeptID
```

FirstName	LastName	Dept Name
Ted	Johnson	Internal Programming
Joann	Wexley	Internal Programming
Alice	Wonderland	External Programming
Tom	Daboss	Marketing
Gary	Moore	HR
Twisted	Sister	Infrastructure
Zack	Wilde	NULL

Figure 27 - OUTER JOIN and results

Even though the statement is written up and down, `LEFT` means the table before the `JOIN` statement and `RIGHT` would refer to table after. In this case the table after the `JOIN` is the primary key table and wouldn't have any NULL values. However table order can be different.

If the table order were reversed a `RIGHT` join would be required to get the same results. This query is shown below in Figure 28 and produces the same results as Figure 27.

```
SELECT E.FirstName, E.LastName,
D.Name AS "Dept Name"
FROM Department D
RIGHT OUTER JOIN
Employee E
ON E.DeptID = D.DeptID
```

Figure 28 - Statement using RIGHT JOIN

For this example the differences in `RIGHT` and `LEFT` and the order of the tables isn't much of an issue. Later when discussing complex multi-table queries it will be shown how order can affect the use of these clauses.

The previously discussed WHERE and ORDER BY clauses can also be used on the end after a JOIN is performed. The following query will take the query of Figure 27 and apply filtering and ordering. Only three rows will be in the results - Wilde, Wonderland, and Wexley, in that order.

```
SELECT E.FirstName, E.LastName,
D.Name AS "Dept Name"
FROM Employee E
LEFT OUTER JOIN
Department D
ON E.DeptID = D.DeptID
WHERE E.LastName LIKE 'W%'
ORDER BY D.Name
```

Figure 29 - Filtering after a JOIN

There is a caveat with the WHERE and ORDER BY clauses. The next query also applies filter and ordering conditions but demonstrates referencing restrictions. Referencing restrictions arise because of the logical processing order of a query which is different from the written order.

Queries are written in the order SELECT FROM WHERE ORDER BY. However when the database processes the statements they are processed in the order FROM WHERE SELECT ORDER BY. This puts limits on where aliases can be referenced. Aliases defined in the FROM can be referenced later because they are defined first, but references defined in SELECT aren't visible when the WHERE clause is processed.

```
SELECT E.FirstName, E.LastName,
D.Name AS "Dept Name"
FROM Employee E
LEFT OUTER JOIN
Department D
ON E.DeptID = D.DeptID
WHERE D.Name LIKE 'In%'
ORDER BY "Dept Name"
```

Figure 30 - Referencing Restrictions

In Figure 30, the WHERE clause is required to access the non-aliased column but the ORDER BY column can use either. This may arise in cases where a query gives an "Invalid column name" if referencing an alias value in the wrong spot.

The JOIN statement isn't limited to only two tables. In fact it is quite common to join several tables together depending on the data that is required.

The next two queries show additional tables. It also is a good example of "building" a query; starting small and adding tables to gather more and more information. It isn't shown below but this method also could also illustrate the usefulness of having a RIGHT or LEFT JOIN depending on where the table is in the query.

```
SELECT E.LastName, P.ProjectName
, P.PercentComplete
FROM Employee E
JOIN EmployeeProject EP
ON E.EmployeeNum = EP.EmployNum
JOIN Project P
ON P.ProjectID = EP.ProjectID
```

```
SELECT E.LastName, P.ProjectName
, P.PercentComplete, WL.Name
FROM Employee E
JOIN EmployeeProject EP
ON E.EmployeeNum = EP.EmployNum
JOIN Project P
ON P.ProjectID = EP.ProjectID
JOIN WorkLocation WL
ON WL.EmployNum = E.EmployeeNum
```

Figure 31 - Multiple tables and query building

The first query in Figure 31 outputs the LastName, ProjectName, and PercentComplete for all Employees with matching projects. The second query adds the Name column from the WorkLocation table. All the techniques discussed above, such as filtering and ordering could be added to further refine the sought after information.

Another common expression found in queries is aggregate functions. These are functions that operate on column values such as SUM(), AVG(), MAX(), etc. Figure 32 shows the simple statement to get the average salary for all Employees.

```
SELECT AVG(E.Salary)
FROM Employee E
```

Figure 32 - Simple Average

This produces a single result – 114285.71 – and has the column data of "(no column name)". Aliasing is required on aggregate column data to have a meaningful name. And while the query is simple, and more practical query would be one that gets the data for a specific Department.

```
SELECT AVG(E.Salary) AS "HR AVG"
FROM Employee E
JOIN Department D
ON E.DeptID = D.DeptID
WHERE D.Name = 'HR'
```

Figure 33 - Practical AVG Query

A common aggregate function is COUNT(). This simply returns the number of rows for the expression. It is written as COUNT(*) and works both with a simple table expression as well as an expression with a filter.

In addition to aliases, statements with aggregate functions also require another clause when including other columns in the result set. This the GROUP BY clause and it makes sense when speaking the stated goal of query out loud. For example to find the average salary per department it is implied that all entries for a department are lumped together to find the average. In SQL this looks like Figure 34.

```
SELECT D.Name AS "Dept Name"
, AVG(E.Salary) AS "Avg Salary"
FROM Department D
JOIN Employee E
ON E.DeptID = D.DeptID
GROUP BY D.Name
```

Figure 34 - GROUP BY clause

As with aliases, the GROUP BY clause has to refer to the original column name because GROUP BY occurs before the SELECT in the logical processing order. In fact, the GROUP BY clause occurs after the WHERE clause, so that means that the aggregation functions (summing/averaging/etc.) occur after the filtering has happened. So to filter on an aggregate (i.e. selecting all rows with an average salary greater than 100000) an additional clause has to be used – HAVING.

HAVING is processed before SELECT but before ORDER BY. So while it must reference the original column names, it can appear in the ORDER BY statement as the aliased name. The query in Figure 35 shows both the use of HAVING and its appearance in the ORDER BY clause.

```
SELECT D.Name AS "Dept Name"
, AVG(E.Salary) AS "Avg Salary"
FROM Department D
JOIN Employee E
ON E.DeptID = D.DeptID
GROUP BY D.Name
HAVING AVG(E.Salary) > 106000
ORDER BY "Avg Salary"
```

Figure 35 - Filtering Aggregations with HAVING

In Figure 32 the query found the average salary of all employees. The result of this query is a single number. This can use used as part of a bigger query. The query shown in Figure 36 finds all Employees with a salary greater than the average salary.

```
SELECT E.Lastname, E.Salary
FROM Employee E
WHERE E.Salary >
(SELECT AVG(E2.Salary)
FROM Employee E2)
```

Figure 36 - Subquery example

When a subquery is used in an expression the results of the subquery must be able to be evaluated as an atomic part of the expression. In the above query a single value is produced so it can be evaluated in a greater than expression. An expression checking for equality would also require a single value. If an expression returned multiple results it would have to be compared using the IN operator.

The query in Figure 36 is known as a non-correlated subquery because the "outer" query and the sub-query do not depend on each other. It can be very inefficient, but sometimes a subquery must be correlated with the outer query. In this case the subquery is executed for each row in the outer query. The query in Figure 37 is a query that selects each employee whose salary is higher than the department average.

To find the department average the subquery calculates the average salary each time a `DeptID` is passed in. Visually the correlated query can be identified by recognizing the two aliases. `E2` is the inner alias and `E` is the outer reference. It can be seen how this is inefficient; for different employees in the same department the entire subquery would be executed separately.

```
SELECT E.LastName, E.Salary
FROM Employee AS E
WHERE E.Salary > (
   SELECT AVG(E2.salary)
   FROM Employee E2
   WHERE E2.DeptID = E.DeptID)
```

Figure 37 - Correlated subquery

Modifying Data

The statements discussed this far (CREATE, INSERT, SELECT) have created tables, inserted data into those tables, and performed various queries to retrieve data from those tables. The final statements to discuss are how to modify data in those tables.

Changing data inside of a table is done with an UPDATE statement. This statement uses a SET clause in the form of `column_name = new_value` to specify a new value for the column. Multiple assignments can be made by using a comma separated list of name/value pairs.

This statement is typically combined with a `WHERE` statement to limit its effect. If the `WHERE` is not included all rows would be updated. All the rules previously described for `WHERE` filters apply here as well.

```
UPDATE Employee
SET Salary = 100001
WHERE EmployeeNum = 22
```

```
UPDATE Employee
SET Salary = Salary + (Salary * 0.10),
FullTime = 1
WHERE EmployeeNum = 44
```

Figure 38 - UPDATE Statements

Notice in the second statement the `SET` statement references itself. This value is referenced as the "before" value. The effect of the second statement above is give the employee a ten percent raise and set them to be a fulltime employee.

To remove rows from a table the `DELETE` statement is used. Again, a `WHERE` statement is used to limit the effect of the statement.

```
DELETE FROM Employee
WHERE EmployeeNum = 100
```

Figure 39 - DELETE Statement

Summary

The previous pages have covered many basic ides of writing SQL statements. Statements for creating both the database and tables were initially demonstrated, and the insert statement to populate those tables was briefly explained. Many forms of the power `SELECT` statement were explained and demonstrated, although the user should also realize that there are a great many forms and combinations of the `SELECT` statement, simply too many to cover in this small introduction. The tables and data have been demonstrably over simplified, however the basics and foundation of what has been shown can be expanded to many practical applications. Databases can regularly have two dozen tables or more but a single query may only deal with a few joins, hence the example database with six tables could easily represent a working subset of a much larger database.

With the basics of SQL statements out of the way, the rest of the book will focus on programming against a database. Different forms of programmatic data manipulation will be shown. Some will use no SQL at all, others may combine language elements and SQL, and a feature known as Language Integrated Query will be demonstrated.

Programming

The SQL statements shown previously are vital for a solid foundation of relational database understanding and troubleshooting. However the majority of applications will access data through a programming framework that, to one degree or another, abstract the specifics of tables and SQL statements away. This section will discuss three .NET frameworks that progressively abstract away the traditional concept of data access.

ADO.NET

The starting point in the .NET world is ADO.Net. This framework provides interfaces and classes that allow basic programmatic access to databases. Note that the term "ADO.Net Provider" may also be used. This is because at its heart ADO.Net is a framework of interfaces that can be implemented by any database vendor. So while Microsoft obviously has implemented the framework for SQL Server there are also providers written for most popular database platforms including Oracle and MySQL. These are downloadable from the vendors themselves.

> NOTE:
> These days ADO.Net is much less popular than other frameworks. It is shown and discussed here because it provides a very nice "transitional bridge" from straight SQL to programming frameworks. Also, a large body of work is out there that may need understood and maintained.

The components of the ADO.Net framework generally fall into the following categories:

Connection – establish and manage a programmatic connection to the database.

Command – encapsulate the SQL statement to execute.

ResultSet – the returned data from the query.

Exception – encapsulates any errors while processing.

The initial interaction between code and database comes in the form of a `Connection` object. This object needs what is known as a "connection string" which contains information about how to physically connect to the database. Each provider can have different information depending on how the perform the connection. While not a complete list the common parts of the SQL Server connection string are shown below.

Server – Name of the database server or (local) if on the same machine.

Database – Name of the database.

User Id – account login (if not integrated)

Password – password for User Id account.

Trusted Connection – True if using Windows
authentication.

The values used are given in name=value pairs separated by
semi-colons. This is typically kept in a configuration file
(web.config for web apps, app.config for
desktop/mobile) and read at runtime. Although discussion
of the configuration system is out of scope for this book a
typical configuration entry is shown in Figure 40.

```
<connectionStrings>
  <add name="AppConnectionString"
    connectionString = "Server=hostServer;
                        Database=JustEnoughDatabase;
                        User Id=test_user;
                        Password=Pa$$w0rd;" />
</connectionStrings>
```

Figure 40 - Example Connection String

Obviously exposing a password directly in a configuration
file is often not advisable. Various schemes exist including
encrypting the password, adding it later, or using only
Windows authentication via
Trusted_Connection=True; instead of the User
Id/Password entries.

Examples in this book will either use a simple configuration
entry like the one above, or hard code the connection string
directly in the source file. These will be done for simplicity
and brevity as the examples will all be simple console
applications.

The examples will be basic C# Windows console applications generated from the standard Windows Console Application project template in Visual Studio. For an application using ADO.NET programmatically all the required libraries and namespaces are available in this project. If additional libraries are needed they will specified.

For a simple console application, even though the libraries are included the namespaces for the various SQL classes must still be imported. For programming against a SQL Server database the built-in SQLClient libraries should be used. The code snippet in Figure 41 actually makes use of three additional namespaces: `System.Data`, `System.Data.Common`, and `System.Data.SqlClient`.

In Figure 41 the code makes use of the interface classes for declaring variables, but instantiates concrete classes from the SqlClient library. This is done mostly for illustrative purposes to show that the ADO.NET library is based on interfaces. Technically the code could be changed to any provider and the variable `conn` could be instantiated with an OracleConnection or MySqlConnection object. There would be similar classes for the other interfaces as well. In most cases this type of flexibility isn't needed and the actual classes are used instead of interface variables.

The output is shown in Figure 42. Following that a discussion of the simple code is shown.

```
static void OutputEmployees(String conString)
{
  IDbConnection conn = new SqlConnection(conString);
  IDbCommand cmd = new SqlCommand(
                    "SELECT * FROM Employee");
  IDataReader dr = null;
  cmd.Connection = conn;

  try
  {
    int id; decimal salary;
    String Lastname, Firstname;
    conn.Open();
    Console.WriteLine("Connection Open!");

    dr = cmd.ExecuteReader();
    while (dr.Read())
    {
      id = dr.GetInt32(0);
      Lastname = dr.GetString(1);
      Firstname = dr.GetString(2);
      salary = dr.GetDecimal(4);

      Console.WriteLine(id + ", " +
          Firstname + " " + Lastname + " " + salary);
    }
  }
  catch (DbException ex)
  {
    Console.WriteLine(ex.StackTrace);
  }
  finally
  {
    if (dr != null) dr.Close();

    conn.Close();
  }
}
```

Figure 41 - Method to print Employee information

```
Connection Open!
22, Ted Johnson 100000.0000
33, Joann Wexley 110000.0000
44, Alice Wonderland 97000.0000
55, Tom Daboss 150000.0000
66, Gary Moore 115000.0000
77, Twisted Sister 107000.0000
88, Zack Wilde 121000.0000
100, To Be Deleted 121100.0000
Press Enter to quit..._
```

Figure 42 - Simple ADO.NET Output

The code in Figure 41 is a complete function taken from a console program. The connection string is specified outside of this function and then passed in; it is simply a string in the exact form shown in Figure 40. The `SqlConnection` object is passed that String in its constructor and will use this later when the `.open()` function is called.

Next a `SqlCommand` object is created with a SQL String as its sole parameter. Notice this String parameter is in exactly the same form as the SQL statements discussed earlier. Also, the Connection property of the `SqlCommand` object is set to the previously declared connection object. This is how the connection and command are tied together.

Inside of the try block, variables are declared that hold our column values, then the connection is opened. Notice that this function has no return value; an exception will be thrown if `open()` fails. More on this in a minute.

To execute the statement and start processing the results the command object's `ExecuteReader()` method is called. There are a few ExecuteXxx() statements and each is named based on the type of object it returns. In this case a `SqlDataReader` (which implements `IDataReader`) is returned and assigned to the `IDataReader` variable.

The `IDataReader.Read()` method is essentially a moving pointer – it points to the next valid record and returns true, or if there are no more records it returns false. At each record a `GetXxx()` method is called and returns the type and value specified by the zero-based index of the columns.

Notice this requires intimate knowledge of the database table and the column order. It also shows why using the "`select *`" syntax could be bad. To be impervious to table changes the statement could have been as shown below with the updated `GetXxx` statements following. These statements would produce the exact same output as Figure 42.

```
IDbCommand cmd = new SqlCommand("SELECT EmployeeNum,
Lastname, FirstName, Salary FROM Employee");

id = dr.GetInt32(0);
Lastname = dr.GetString(1);
Firstname = dr.GetString(2);
salary = dr.GetDecimal(3);
```

Figure 43 - Specified Columns in SqlCommand

Some general notes about the code in Figure 41:

- Database function calls should always be in the `try/catch/finally` block as exceptions are thrown when errors occur.
- The `catch` block should catch a `DbException` object or an object derived from `DbException` (such as `SqlException`).
- The `finally` block should clean up resources if they are open. Behind the scenes ADO.NET opens actual system resources (such as file handles and memory) and a call to `Close()` is required to let the system know when they are no longer needed.

It was mentioned before that there is a small family of `ExecuteXxx()` functions. These are detailed next. It should be noted that the `ExecuteXxx()` calls are 'blocking' calls, meaning that the function has to return before the program continues. So an `ExecuteReader()` that returns one million rows has to go to the database, execute the complete query, and send back the entire data set before processing of them begins. Depending on the query and the data the time for that could be substantial. There are also asynchronous versions of all of these functions. These allow for the query to be started and a callback function to be called when the query is complete. Discussion of the asynchronous programming pattern is beyond the scope of this book but it can be an important option in time- or resource-critical applications.

`ExecuteNonQuery` – This function is mainly used for Insert, Update, and Delete statements. The return value is the number of rows affected. Other uses could be statements to create tables or other database objects programmatically. Figure 44 shows the code to delete a row in the Employee Table. The output would be "1 row deleted!"

```
static void DeleteEmployee100(String conString)
{
    IDbConnection conn = new SqlConnection(conString);
    IDbCommand cmd = new SqlCommand("DELETE Employee
                        WHERE EmployeeNum = 100");

    cmd.Connection = conn;

    try
    {
        conn.Open();
        Console.WriteLine("Connection Open!");

        int count = cmd.ExecuteNonQuery();

        Console.WriteLine(count + " row(s) deleted!");
    }
    catch (SqlException ex)
    {
        Console.WriteLine(ex.StackTrace);
    }
    finally
    {
        conn.Close();
    }
}
```

Figure 44 - Delete with ExecuteNonQuery

`ExecuteScalar` – return a single value from the query. Technically this function returns the first column of the first row and ignores the rest, so even if the query produces multiple rows and values only one will be returned. The return value is of type object and must be cast to the desired type. Figure 45 shows simplified statements (all supporting code removed) to return different types.

```
IDbCommand cmd = new SqlCommand("SELECT COUNT(*)
                                From Employee");
int count = (int)cmd.ExecuteScalar();
Console.WriteLine(count + " Employee Rows.");


IDbCommand cmd = new SqlCommand("SELECT LastName
                FROM Employee WHERE EmployeeNum = 22");
String lname = (String)cmd.ExecuteScalar();
Console.WriteLine(lname + " is the first employee.");
```

Figure 45 - ExecuteScalar Examples

The output from each of these would be "8 Employee Rows" and "Johnson is the first employee" respectively. Notice how each result is cast to the desired type.

Providers may have implementation-specific `ExecuteXxx` methods as well. For example the SqlClient implementation has an `ExecuteXmlReader` function because MS Sql Server has the ability to render a query in XML format. These commands will not be discussed or detailed here. Any implementation-specific code will have to be further researched by the reader if needed.

Thus far the SQL queries have had the selection values hard-coded in the query string. This is clearly untenable for a real system; there is no way of knowing up front what the actual EmployeeNum values would be. And how would a search on strings work?

One way would be to use a class such as `StringBuilder` to dynamically build a string. Figure 46 shows an example of building this type of statement.

```
StringBuilder sb = new StringBuilder();
sb.Append("SELECT LastName FROM
           Employee WHERE EmployeeNum = ");
sb.Append(EmpID);

SqlCommand cmd = new SqlCommand(sb.ToString());
```

Figure 46 - Dynamically build SQL String

Even though the code in Figure 46 looks straight forward and simple, BUILDING DYNAMIC SQL STATEMENTS LIKE THAT SHOULD **NEVER** BE DONE IN REAL CODE. This is because dynamic SQL is a huge security risk due to something known as a SQL Injection Attack. In that attack malicious statements are included with the included SQL and then executed blindly by the database engine.

The proper way to create queries such that they can accept input is to use parameters. This is essentially putting a placeholder in the query at compile time and having the framework supply a real value at run time. The concept of parameters is widely supported among database vendors but the syntax varies between them; the statements and upcoming examples are specific to SQL server syntax.

In SQL Server a parameter is a variable prefixed with the "@" symbol. This tells both the database engine and the framework where the placeholders are located.

```
static void FindEmployee(String conString, int EmpID)
{

    SqlCommand cmd = new SqlCommand("SELECT LastName
             FROM Employee WHERE EmployeeNum = @EmpNum");

    SqlParameter parm = new SqlParameter("@EmpNum", EmpID);
    cmd.Parameters.Add(parm);

    // rest of code remains the same

}
```

Figure 47 - Using a parameter

A new object is introduced – SqlParameter. It is constructed with both a name and value. It is then added to a Command object collection property called Parameters. All parameters used for a particular command need to be constructed and added in this way.

Notice that the name given to it matches the name of the parameter in the statement. This is important when there are many parameters present and allows the framework to easily match each parameter to its proper placeholder. At runtime the framework logically replaces each parameter with the given value and executes the final statement. It also enforces type safety and performs security checks on each parameter to eliminate SQL injection.

DataSets

The code for ADO.NET thus far is often referred to as "connected mode" code because all the data is processed during an active connection. This is mainly ideal for small, quick queries such as list population and display of read-only information. Although `UPDATE` and `INSERT` commands can be specified in `SqlCommand` statements this can often time require a lot of change detection logic with large data sets.

ADO.NET has objects that allow for processing offline while also maintaining the structure of the database, or building a structure completely in code and then persisting to a database platform when finished. Unlike the manual statements above these objects also can perform change detection and use a simplified update/insert strategy. These objects, the center of which is the `DataSet`, also allow for easy interaction with graphical data display elements such as `DataTable` and `DropDownList` controls.

A key object between the `DataSet` and the actual data is the `DataAdapter`. This object handles the behind-the-scenes managing of the data and knows how to pull and push data between the data source and the `DataSet`. The code example below in Figure 48 shows a basic wiring of data in a simple Windows Forms application. Without going in detail surrounding Windows Forms there is basically a `DataGridView` control (named dgvEmployees) with a `DataSource` property.

Many Forms, WPF, and Web Grid controls have a similar property so this type of "wiring together" works for many other controls as well. When loaded the adapter connects to the database, retrieves the data, and populates the view as shown in Figure 49.

```csharp
private void Form1_Load(object sender, EventArgs e)
{
    try
    {
        SqlConnection conn =
            new SqlConnection(GetConnectionString());
        SqlDataAdapter da =
            new SqlDataAdapter("SELECT * FROM Employee",
                               conn);

        DataSet ds = new DataSet();
        da.Fill(ds);

        dgvEmployees.DataSource = ds.Tables[0];
    }
    catch(SqlException ex)
    {
        MessageBox.Show(
            "Error connecting to database: " + ex.Message,
            "Connection Error");
    }
}
```

Figure 48 - Simple DataAdapter and DataSet

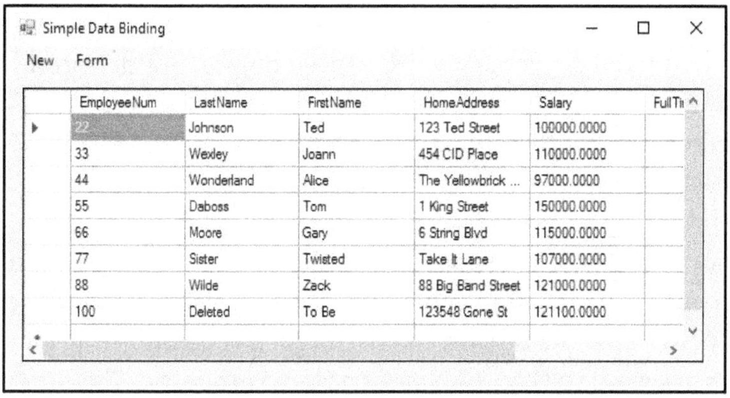

EmployeeNum	LastName	FirstName	HomeAddress	Salary	FullTi
22	Johnson	Ted	123 Ted Street	100000.0000	
33	Wexley	Joann	454 CID Place	110000.0000	
44	Wonderland	Alice	The Yellowbrick ...	97000.0000	
55	Daboss	Tom	1 King Street	150000.0000	
66	Moore	Gary	6 String Blvd	115000.0000	
77	Sister	Twisted	Take It Lane	107000.0000	
88	Wilde	Zack	88 Big Band Street	121000.0000	
100	Deleted	To Be	123548 Gone St	121100.0000	

Figure 49 - Results of Simple Data Binding

Notice in Figure 48 that the `DataSource` is set to an object in the `Tables` collection of the `DataSet` object `ds`. This further reinforces the notion that a `DataSet` can have many tables. In this code example there is only one table in the DataSet, but code could be put in place to replicate and load the entire database into a single DataSet. Then each table could be referenced by name, such as `ds.Tables["Project"]` or `ds.Tables["Department"]`.

Using the methods in Figure 48 is only a slight step above the connected code. The `DataAdapter` is taking care of the connection `Open()` and `Close()` methods, but otherwise the data is being retrieved and then simply viewed. Using the framework in a truly disconnected mode requires a little more work.

Figure 50 has an example of the code required to make truly disconnected processing work. Three objects are declared at the Form level so they can be referenced in different methods. Essentially, when the form loads it creates an instance of the `DataAdapter` and declares its structure with the `SELECT * FROM Employee` statement. What is not immediately obvious is that the `DataAdapter` has a separate property for each action; when passing a command in the `SqlDataAdapter` constructor the passed-in string gets assigned to the `SelectCommand` property. This allows the `Fill()` method to populate a DataSet but does not allow for any other operation through the adapter back to the original database data. The other properties, `UpdateCommand`, `InsertCommand`, and `DeleteCommand` must be populated before any modified data can be saved back to the database.

```
SqlDataAdapter _adapter = null;
DataSet _ds = new DataSet();
SqlConnection _conn = null;

private void Form3_Load(object sender, EventArgs e)
{
    _conn = new SqlConnection(GetConnectionString());
    _adapter = new SqlDataAdapter("SELECT * FROM Employee",
                                 _conn);

    _adapter.Fill(_ds);
    dgvEditEmployees.DataSource = _ds.Tables[0];
    _conn.Close();

}

private void btnSave_Click(object sender, EventArgs e)
{
    DataSet changes = _ds.GetChanges();
```

```
SqlCommandBuilder builder =
            new SqlCommandBuilder(_adapter);
_adapter.UpdateCommand = builder.GetUpdateCommand();
_adapter.InsertCommand = builder.GetInsertCommand();
_adapter.DeleteCommand = builder.GetDeleteCommand();

_conn.Open();
_adapter.Update(changes);
_conn.Close();

}
```

Figure 50 - Disconnected Editing and Saving

The DataSet keeps track of which objects are changed and exposes them via a GetChanges() method. Each row in the changes set can be a modified existing row, new row, or a row that has been deleted. This will determine how the Update() method handles each row.
There are a couple ways to populate the remaining XxxCommand properties of the adapter. One is to manually write the SQL statements and assign them to each property. This is often overwhelming and error prone. In Figure 50 an easier way is shown – using the library's SqlCommandBuilder object. The adapter's initial command is shown to be a SELECT * FROM Employee. The SqlCommandBuilder will examine that statement and construct a corresponding statements when each GetXxxCommand() is called. Once those commands are generated and assigned, the connection is reopened, the changes will be applied, and the connection closed again.

As an example of how complex the generated statement can be the actual text from the `UpdateCommand` statement in Figure 50 is shown below. The statement has a large number of variables because each column value can potentially be changed, and to correctly identify the row to update each column value is compared with the original value.

```
UPDATE [Employee] SET [EmployeeNum] = @p1, [LastName] =
@p2, [FirstName] = @p3, [HomeAddress] = @p4, [Salary] =
@p5, [FullTime] = @p6, [DeptID] = @p7 WHERE (([EmployeeNum]
= @p8) AND ([LastName] = @p9) AND ([FirstName] = @p10) AND
([HomeAddress] = @p11) AND ([Salary] = @p12) AND
([FullTime] = @p13) AND ((@p14 = 1 AND [DeptID] IS NULL) OR
([DeptID] = @p15)))
```

Figure 51 - UPDATE SqlCommand from the DataAdapter

As another bridge towards modern ORM technologies a wizard-generated Dataset will now be shown. This is also known as creating a typed DataSet because the database structure is examined and a XSD schema file is created to ensure type safety. In this manner no code is needed to be written by the developer; all references to the data are through objects.

The following description will be in the context of a Visual Studio Windows project. However a typed dataset can be used in any sort of project including library and we projects. It can also be coded by hand as the entire typed dataset definition is simply an XSD schema file and some supporting definition files. This would be extremely tedious and error prone and is usually discouraged.

The option to create a dataset and add it to the project is simply chosen by right-clicking on the project and selecting Add->New Item and then Data->DataSet. This will create a new XSD file and launch a blank design surface screen. Once a data connection is set up in the Server Explorer the objects from the connected database can simply be drag-and-dropped onto the design surface.

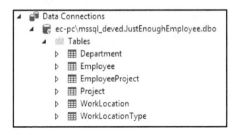

Figure 52 - Server Explorer View

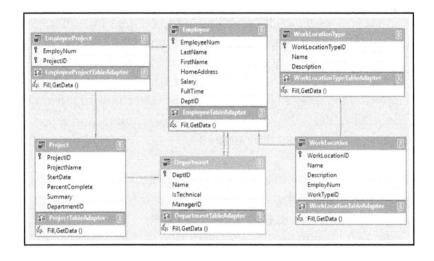

Figure 53 - DataSet Design Surface

Figure 53 shows the design surface after all the tables from the database have been added. Note that each object is represented by both the `DataTable` object and its respective `DataAdapter`. The design surface logic has taken care to examine each object and create the associated adapter with all commands already built in. The XSD file would be quite extensive, and there would also be a generated c-sharp language file to declare all of the class-based code that derives from the Framework code which the programmer will use. In the upcoming examples the generated code for the `DataSet`-derived is in a class named `CompleteDataSet`.

With all these objects defined filling the DataGridView is simple. No SQL is needed from the programmer.

```
ProjectTableAdapter pta = new ProjectTableAdapter();
CompleteDataSet ds = new CompleteDataSet();
pta.Fill(ds.Project);
dgvProjects.DataSource = ds.Project;
```

Figure 54 - Using Generated DataSet Objects

Notice in Figure 53 that the design surface has picked up and displays the relations between the tables, just as in the ER diagram earlier in the book. This allows for the programmatic navigation between objects that are related. This can be useful in master/detail scenarios or screens where combined information is shown.

For example if a screen was constructed to show the details of an employee, including their department name and the number of projects they were associated with, the following code would get that information (hardcoded as the first employee just for demonstration purposes).

```
EmployeeTableAdapter eta = new EmployeeTableAdapter();
DepartmentTableAdapter dta = new DepartmentTableAdapter();
EmployeeProjectTableAdapter epta =
                  new EmployeeProjectTableAdapter();

CompleteDataSet ds = new CompleteDataSet();
eta.Fill(ds.Employee);
dta.Fill(ds.Department);
epta.Fill(ds.EmployeeProject);

CompleteDataSet.EmployeeRow er = ds.Employee[0];

String Lastname = er.LastName;
String Firstname = er.FirstName;
```

```
String DeptName = er.DepartmentRow.Name;

int numProjects = er.GetEmployeeProjectRows().Count();
```

Figure 55 - Using Data Relations

Notice that multiple adapters are used to fill their respective tables in the DataSet. This has implications also if the screen would allow editing; each adapter would have to update its respective table as well. Depending on the operation (update/insert/delete) the ordering may be important. For example if inserting new entities the "child" entity would have to be inserted first so that the "parent" entity could use the new id value. So while knowledge of the table structure and relations is important actual SQL code would not have to be written.

The discussion so far has shown limited code snippets and a pretty high-level description of the ADO.NET technology. This is because although it may be seen in production code and possibly even used for brand new small projects, in general it is somewhat dated technology. Based on the basic examples and the code shown one should be able to pick up missing details in existing code.

The following discussion on Entity Framework will be more in-depth because it will most likely be the technology of choice for recent and new .NET projects. A general discussion of the technology is presented first, followed by a detailed discussion of both creating and using the model.

Entity Framework

The latest in .NET ORM technology is the Entity Framework (EF). There are actually several ways to use EF, in general these are referred to as "Code First" and "Database First" although Microsoft has also recently added the peculiarly named compromise "Code First from a Database" into the mix.

The approach of "Database First" is similar to the `DataSet` approach. Essentially an existing database is analyzed via a wizard and/or designer and object classes representing the structure are created from that. This may be common in enterprise development where there are rules concerning database design and deployment, or where there is an existing legacy database to work with.

The difference from the XSD approach is that instead of working with `DataSets`, `TableAdapters`, `DataRows`, and other framework objects, there are higher-level abstractions created and the programmer is working with domain objects and collections more frequently than objects based on Framework classes. Tables are represented as classes, columns as properties of that class, and related entities as properties or collections. Generic classes and collections are used extensively to foster this paradigm.

In the "Code First" approach, the entire database structure is model in classes. Again, tables are a fully contained classes with columns as properties. When a connection is made to a database server, the framework detects whether the actual database objects exist. If not, they are created. If the definitions have changed the database can also be updated. In this way the user technically never has to use any database software to maintain the database.

To demonstrate the "Database First" operation a simple console application will be used. Keep in mind that in a real system the data modeling and data access code would most likely be in a library (dll) project to promote reuse. Here the data model will be included in the project for simplicity.

After creating a console project, the next step is to add a new item to the project. Right clicking on the project and selected Add->New Item->Data. A new Entity Data Model is selected with the choice of "ADO.NET Entity Data Model" and specifying a name – "SimpleEmployee" as shown in the figure below (entire dialog not shown; only the relevant sections).

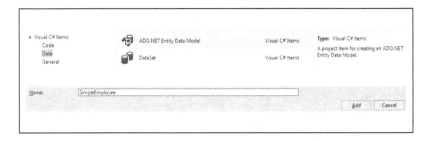

Figure 56 - New Data Item (Entity Data Model)

Once the name is chosen a wizard is started. There are several choices as shown in Figure 57. The last one, "Code First From a Database" will be described later. "EF Designer from database" will be stepped through to design the basic data model.

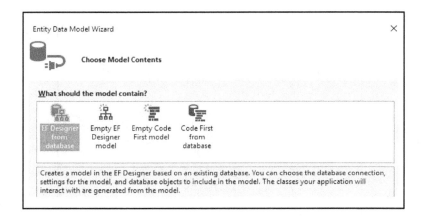

Figure 57 - Choosing EF Designer

The next step is the wizard is to choose a connection to a database. This can be an existing or a new connection and the full connection string along with some additional metadata will be stored. Notice that in this case the connection string will be saved to the config file.

The name that it is given will also be the name of the Entity class inside of the code. While the amount of framework related classes in much less than with ADO.NET Datasets, the highest level abstraction in EF will be still be an Entity and other classes will be contained within that.

The next wizard step is simply for selecting the version of the Framework. Unless there is a need for a previous version the latest version should always be selected. This step will not be shown as it may be changes or removed based on the versions supported.

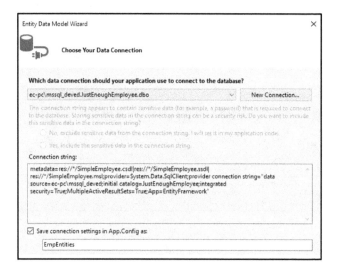

Figure 58 - Specifying a connection

Once the Framework version is chosen the next wizard step is to choose the objects to import into the model. Figure 59 shows the objects in the database grouped into three areas – tables, views, and stored procedures. Although they haven't been discussed heretofore, views can best be thought of a "virtual" tables. In general they are used for read-only datasets that may aggregate data from multiple tables, but are presented in a single table-like format with rows and columns.

Stored procedures are SQL statements that are stored within the database. While not covered in the previous section on SQL statements, it is enough here to understand that they would be mapped as functions in the data modeling world. There are none in this database however, so no mapping will occur.

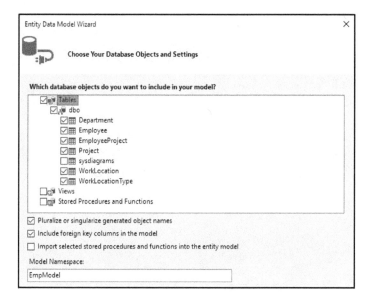

Figure 59 - Selecting Database objects for the model

All the database tables will be brought into the model into the namespace specified by the "Model Namespace" setting. It is also important to discuss the checkbox "Pluralize or singularize generated object names." This will make the collections plural and try to figure out other places where singular and plural tenses should be used.

Once the objects are chosen the model will be generated. The image in Figure 60 shows the files in the solution in Visual Studio. Not all of the files will be discussed but it is important to understand several pieces of information.

Figure 60 - Simple Employee Entity Data Model

First, the `EmpEntities` class is the "container" for all other classes. It is the "entry point" into the data model. That class handles the connection to and manages all other interaction with the database backend. Notice that it makes extensive use of derived template classes so that domain objects appear as normal object collections.

The `Employees` class is derived from `DbSet<Employee>`, `Department` from `DbSet<Department>`, and so on. `DbSet` is the base class that allows the ease of manipulation. The data classes will be discussed soon.

Secondly, `EmpEntities` has properties for all the constituent tables in the database. Notice two things about these properties – they are plural (because that was specified in the wizard) and they are generic collections with a parameter type of a class that is defined toward the bottom of the model.

Third, the SimpleEmployee.tt object is actually made up of classes that represent the individual record types in the database. These are the types for the collection properties above and exist to model each table in the database. The code for the Employee model is shown in Figure 61 (some attributes removed for clarity).

```
public partial class Employee
{
    public Employee()
    {
        this.Departments = new HashSet<Department>();
        this.WorkLocations = new HashSet<WorkLocation>();
        this.Projects = new HashSet<Project>();
    }

    public int EmployeeNum { get; set; }
    public string LastName { get; set; }
    public string FirstName { get; set; }
    public string HomeAddress { get; set; }
    public decimal Salary { get; set; }
    public bool FullTime { get; set; }
    public Nullable<int> DeptID { get; set; }
```

```
    public virtual ICollection<Department>
          Departments { get; set; }

    public virtual Department Department { get; set; }

    public virtual ICollection<WorkLocation>
          WorkLocations { get; set; }

    public virtual ICollection<Project>
          Projects { get; set; }
}
```

Figure 61 - Employee Class Definition

In this simple class each column in the database is represented as a simple public property. The related Department is represented by both a `DeptID` property that has only the Id value, and the `Department` property which will return the associated `Department`. The `Departments` collection is for navigating backwards because there is also a relationship from `Departments` to `Employee` for the `ManagerID` field.

Before demonstrating how the entities are actually used in code, it is worth noting what is missing from the model. When comparing the boxes checked in Figure 59 to the classes in Figure 60 it is apparent that the table `EmployeeProject` was not included in the model. This is because the framework was actually clever enough to figure out the purpose of that table and model a many-to-many relationship as collections in both entities.

So in Figure 61 there is a collection property
(ICollection<Project> Projects) for the many
projects associated with an Employee. Similarly in the
Project class there is an ICollection<Employee>
Employees property for the many employees associated
to a Project.

Using the Entity Data Model in code is very simple. The
code below shows a very simple loop to print information to
the console.

```
private static void ShowEmployeeInfo()
{
    EmpEntities ent = new EmpEntities();
    foreach (Employee e in ent.Employees)
    {
        Console.WriteLine("Employee: " + e.FirstName +
                          " " + e.LastName);
        Console.WriteLine("is in " +
          (e.DeptID.HasValue ? e.Department.Name : "no") +
          " Department");

        Console.WriteLine();
    }
}
```

Figure 62 - EF Model Usage

As another example the many-to-many relationship by using
simple collections is shown below in Figure 63.

```
private static void ShowEmployeeProjects()
{
    EmpEntities ent = new EmpEntities();

    foreach (Employee e in ent.Employees)
    {
        Console.WriteLine("Employee: " + e.FirstName +
                          " " + e.LastName);

        Console.WriteLine("has " + e.Projects.Count +
                          " projects.");

        if (e.Projects.Count > 0)
        {
            foreach (Project p in e.Projects)
            {
                Console.WriteLine("\tProject: " +
                                  p.ProjectName);
            }
        }
    }
}
```

Figure 63 - Collections Properties for Relations

Thus far the collections have been read-only and there hasn't been any modifications to the data. However since the column values are simply properties the value can be updated with a simple assignment statement. When the changes are ready to be committed back to the database the SaveChanges() method on the entity object is called. Note that this operation can throw an exception for various reasons including invalid data. The code doesn't show exception handling but it should always be included.

```
private static void GiveEveryoneARaise()
{
    EmpEntities ent = new EmpEntities();

    foreach (Employee e in ent.Employees)
    {
        e.Salary += 2500;
    }

    ent.SaveChanges();
}
```

Figure 64 - Updating values and SaveChanges()

So far the data has been read from the table and accessed, and even updated. But the tables have been read in total – no filtering has been done. If the entire database structure is represented as a set of classes and collections how is querying and filtering to be done? This is where a powerful new concept has been introduced – Language Integrated Query, or LINQ for short.

Language Integrated Query (LINQ)

LINQ makes querying a first-class citizen in the code world. Rather than having to write a SQL statement as a string and passing that into some sort of execute query method, functions, expressions, and lambdas are used to construct filters directly in code. The Entity Framework takes care of the behind-the-scenes conversion to SQL syntax and execution. And although it is possible to pass in a hand-crafted SQL string the framework methods often result in more efficient code.

The first type of expression to be discussed in known as Fluent Syntax. It relies on filter methods and lambda expressions to perform its filtering. Essentially these methods are extension methods on the collection classes that allow for Boolean expressions to perform the filtering. Full explanation of extension methods and lambda syntax will not be included here, only what is necessary to demonstrate Fluent LINQ.

One thing to note is that the extension methods return an instance of a generic interface – `IEnumerable<T>`. This interface allows for "chaining" of the methods together, hence the fluent syntax. It also allows for delayed execution and requires a conversion at the end which will be demonstrated and discussed in the examples.

```
EmpEntities emp = new EmpEntities();

// Basic LINQ Where query
IEnumerable<Employee> highPaid =
    emp.Employees.Where(e => e.Salary > 110000);

foreach (Employee e in highPaid)
{
    Console.WriteLine(e.LastName + " is overpaid!");
}
```

Figure 65 - LINQ Basic Where Query

Figure 65 shows a very basic LINQ query, but several important observations need to be discussed. Notice that the .Where() method is called directly on the Employees property of the entities object.
Recall from earlier that Employees is actually a class derived from DbSet<Employee> and represents a collection of objects. The Where method uses a lambda expression "e => e.Salary > 110000" to filter the set. In lambda syntax, "e" is the declaration of the variable, and the expression on the right side of the double arrow is applied to each element in the collection. If true then the element is part of the filtered set.

For each query the original set isn't modified, rather a new set is returned. The objects in the new set can be modified and saved back to the database if desired. All values in the objects in both collections are simple properties and can be read or updated as described previously.

NOTE: the foreach loop code will not be repeated in the upcoming snippets unless vastly different from Figure 65. In Figure 65 the resultant object is of type IEnumerable<Employee>. This implies that the result of the Where() function, an IEnumerable list itself, could also have a function called on it. This is what allows for the "Fluent" syntax to get its name. Multiple operations on the same dataset can be fluently chained together. This code executes the same query but also orders the results.

```
IEnumerable<Employee> IEList = emp.Employees
                    .Where(x => x.Salary > 110000)
                    .OrderBy(o => o.Salary);
```

Figure 66 - Fluent multiple methods

There are many other additional query functions that can be used to perform SQL-like operations on the objects. The following table lists a few of the common operations. Some return collections that can have further operations applied to them while some return either a single object or number. A complete listing is available in the MSDN documentation.

Take(int n)	Returns only the first n values of the results.
Skip(int n)	Skips the first n values and returns the rest of the results.
Distinct()	Removed duplicates from the results.

`ThenBy(exp)`	Used for secondary ordering; after OrderBy, ThenBy, etc.
`First()`	Returns the first result.
`FirstOrDefault()`	Returns the first or a default object if results are empty.
`Last()`	Returns the last object in the result set.
`Count()`	Returns the number of records in the result set.

One operator that is missing from the above grid is the `Select()` operator. This operator has many different ways to be used and will be a discussion all on its own.

In the queries thus far the `Select()` function was implied. However it can be explicitly included, but after reviewing the syntax it is obvious why it can be omitted. The generated list and output of Figure 67 below is identical to the output of the code in Figure 66.

```
IEnumerable<Employee> orderedOverPaid = emp.Employees
                    .Where(x => x.Salary > 110000)
                    .OrderBy(o => o.Salary)
                    .Select(n => n);
```

Figure 67 - Select() an entire object

A more common use of Select() is to return only the desired properties of the object. For single values the return type is easily identifiable and can be code quite easily. Since the LastName property is a String the results of the query will be a collection of strings. Figure 68 shows the use of the Select() operation to select a single property.

```
IEnumerable<String> orderedLastNames = emp.Employees
                        .Where(e =>e.Salary > 110000)
                        .OrderBy(e => e.Salary)
                        .Select(e => e.LastName);

foreach (String str in orderedLastNames)
{
    Console.WriteLine(str + " is overpaid!");
}
```

Figure 68 - Selecting only a single property

Note that if the return type can be determined, the Select() operation can have a more complex expression. For example (e => e.FirstName + " " + e.LastName) would still result in a collection of Strings.

It is often not good practice to perform those type of transformations in the query itself. It is a better solution to create a new type that represent the desired fields and use the Select() operator to transform the results into a new type. With a new type defined in Figure 69, the query in Figure 70 will transform the results to the new type and then use the new type in the output statement.

Transforming to a new type can be very useful for adapting subsets of data to the desired need. For example many types of GUI controls such as dropdown lists can only use two values – an Id and a DisplayName. Using the `Select()` operator to retrieve only the usable data from a much larger set is very useful in that scenario.

```csharp
public class SimplePerson
{
    public int PersonId { get; set; }
    public String FullName { get; set; }
    public Decimal Salary { get; set; }
}
```

Figure 69 - New SimplePerson

```csharp
IEnumerable<SimplePerson> peeps = emp.Employees
                .Where(e => (e.Salary > 110000))
                .OrderBy(e => e.Salary)
                .Select(e => new SimplePerson
                {
                    PersonId = e.EmployeeNum,
                    Salary = e.Salary,
                    FullName = e.FirstName + " " +
                                e.LastName
                });
foreach (SimplePerson sp in peeps)
{
    Console.WriteLine(sp.FullName + " is highly paid: " +
                String.Format("{0:C}", sp.Salary));
}
```

Figure 70 - Using Select to transform to a new class

The final type of projection with the Select() operation involves creating new anonymous types. This is quite often used and actually requires the use of the var keyword, as the actually type of the query will not be known to the programmer. The compiler figures it all out and gives the type an internal name.

```
var orderedPair = emp.Employees
                    .Where(x => x.Salary > 110000)
                    .OrderBy(o => o.Salary)
                    .Select(n => new
                    {
                        id = n.EmployeeNum,
                        Name = n.LastName
                    });

foreach (var v in orderedPair)
{
    Console.WriteLine(v.Name + "(" + v.id + ")" +
                    " is anonymously overpaid!");
}
```

Figure 71 - new anonymous type

One thing that is not so apparent about the queries so far is that LINQ actually uses delayed execution for its queries. That means that the statement above in Figure 66 actually doesn't bring back any results, it simply defines the query. LINQ will not go the database and get data until it needs to, which is defined as the first time the result needs to be accessed. In Figure 56 the query actually will not execute and bring back results until the foreach loop is entered.

In certain cases it is desirable to load the results immediately. This is often done to load the results directly into a list. Sometimes programming style also prefers this as results are loaded directly into a List variable and manipulated using the collection classes rather than the IEnumarble interface. Understanding when the query is executed however is important. Figure 72 shows the syntax for using executing immediately using ToList().

```
List<Employee> orderedHPList= emp.Employees
                    .Where(x => x.Salary > 110000)
                    .OrderBy(o => o.Salary)
                    .ToList();
```

Figure 72 - Immediate query execution, stored in a List

Delayed execution is not something that is normally thought about, it is more a "behind the scenes" performance issue. It also has implications when accessing object properties that refer to other tables (such as in Figure 62) but there again it can usually be ignored except for certain performance issues. Essentially the related objects (such as Department) are not loaded when Employee is loaded; the framework only goes and gets them when they are accessed (known as "Lazy Loading").

Although Lazy loading is the default, there are two ways to load related objects when the running the query, both of which themselves have options of how to implement. All options must be considered carefully as related object loading will always have a performance cost and tradeoffs should be examined.

Explicit loading can be written into the query such that when the query is executed the specified related entity is also retrieved and populated. The framework has an `Include()` method that allows the programmer to specify the name of the related object. By default the string argument is the only method; however by setting a project reference to the `System.Data.Entity` assembly additional overloaded Include() methods are available.

```
// Original way - using string to specify
List<Employee> empList =
        ent.Employees.Include("Department").ToList();

// Must include reference to System.Data.Entity
//and using statement
List<Employee> empListLambda =
    ent.Employees.Include(e => e.Department).ToList();
```

Figure 73 - Explicitly loading related entities

Eager loading can be set multiple ways as well. One will be discussed later in the Code First section; here the property-based method will be shown. There is a property on the entity object that tells the framework to load any related objects when any `DbSet` is loaded. That property is set immediately after creation as shown in Figure 74. For any collection loaded in the database its first level relations will also be loaded.

```
EmpEntities ent = new EmpEntities();
ent.Configuration.LazyLoadingEnabled = false;

List<Employee> empList = ent.Employees.ToList();

foreach (Employee e in empList)
{
    Console.WriteLine("Employee: " + e.FirstName +
                " " + e.LastName);
    Console.WriteLine("is in " +
        (e.DeptID.HasValue ? e.Department.Name : "no") +
        " Department");
}
```

Figure 74 - Disabling Lazy Loading via an Entities Property

Before moving to joining tables together, which honestly looks a little strange in Fluent syntax, the other type of LINQ query will be discussed. Query Syntax (or Query Expressions) is another form of writing expressions and can sometimes present a better picture of the query's intention. Part of the appeal also is that it follows the logical query order which was discussed back in the beginnings of the query section.

One thing to note is that the choice between Fluent and Query Expression is both stylistic and pragmatic. Behind the scenes the compiler will translate Query Syntax into Fluent syntax (Albahari, 2016) because everything is an object and the compiler sees things best as a series of function calls. The programmer however may find it easier to understand one or the other and can use whichever is clearest. There are also methods that aren't supported in Query Syntax so those queries would either be written in Fluent Syntax or in a query that combines the two styles (Albahari, 2016).

Query Syntax

Query Syntax often makes the most sense to those who have been working in raw SQL for a long time. Even though the order of the statements appear backwards they closely follow the logical order of SQL processing. This was discussed earlier in the section on raw SQL. An example that compares Fluent and Query Syntax is shown in Figure 75. The Fluent query is included for reference; both queries produce the exact same list of records.

Also from Figure 75 it is evident how Query Syntax mimics the logical order of SQL. The 'from' statement is first which identifies the data elements, then the filter, then the select. In upcoming examples this will be expanded on to show other operations.

It should also be noted in Figure 75 that the full type of the result, `IEnumerable<Employee>`, is specified. It is common practice to shorten this using `var` in query syntax and the rest of the examples will use the shorted version.

```
EmpEntities emp = new EmpEntities();

// Figure 65
IEnumerable<Employee> highPaidFluent =
            emp.Employees.Where(e => e.Salary > 110000);


IEnumerable<Employee> highPaid = from e in emp.Employees
                              where e.Salary > 110000
                              select e;
foreach (var theEmp in highPaid)
{
    Console.WriteLine(theEmp.LastName +
                " is overpaid accoding to QE!");
}

foreach (var theEmp in highPaidFluent)
{
    Console.WriteLine(theEmp.LastName +
                " is overpaid accoding to Fluent!");
}
```

Figure 75 - Fluent and Query Syntax

Adding additional clauses is also straight forward. Next is a
Query Expression that includes an order clause. It also uses
projection to create a new type by only picking parts of the
object to create an anonymous type. Even though it is a
convention even when the type is known, in this case use of
var is required because just as in Figure 71 the resultant
type is named by the compiler.

```
EmpEntities emp = new EmpEntities();

var query = from e in emp.Employees
            where e.Salary > 110000
            orderby e.LastName
            select new {
                            e.LastName,
                            e.Salary,
                            e.Department
                        };

foreach(var hp in query)
{
    Console.WriteLine(hp.LastName +
                " is highly paid - " + hp.Salary);
}
```

Figure 76 - Order and Projection in a Query Expression

Query Syntax will arguably satisfy a large number of data access query requirements. Since it is built in to the language use of variables is also straight forward. Rather than hard-coding the value in a variable could have been used (i.e. where e.Salary > bigSal); however this applies equally to Fluent and Query Syntax.

One of the primary reasons to use Query Syntax is for the ease with which join conditions are coded. This looks very much like the join in raw SQL and allows the programmer to clearly state the conditions for joining. Figure 77 shows how to join two collections based on common fields. While this requires knowledge of the common properties, Visual Studio helps because by dealing with objects there is intellisense available to suggest fields. In contrast the equivalent Fluent Syntax is shown in Figure 78.

```
EmpEntities emp = new EmpEntities();

var query = from e in emp.Employees
            join d in emp.Departments
            on e.DeptID equals d.DeptID
            select new { e.LastName, d.Name };

foreach (var emps in query)
{
    Console.WriteLine(emps.LastName + " is in " +
                      emps.Name + " Department");
}
```

Figure 77 - Query Syntax JOIN statement

```
var query = emp.Employees.Join(
    emp.Departments,
    e => e.DeptID,
    d => d.DeptID,
    (e, d) => new { e.LastName, d.Name }
);
```

Figure 78 - Fluent equivalent JOIN statement

Comparing Figures 77 and 78 it is readily seen how Query Syntax is more intuitive than Fluent Syntax when joining entities. Fluent syntax (Figure 79) uses the `Join` function as an extension method on one collection with several lambda expressions as arguments. In order they are the collection to join, the first collection key to join on, the second collection key to compare, and the selection function.

The use of lambdas is not terribly inconvenient, but the Fluent Syntax quickly becomes very verbose and cluttered when adding additional tables. Figure 79 below shows a query with multiple tables joined together, an `orderby` clause, and selecting into a new anonymous type. While this would be possible with Fluent Syntax it would be much more verbose and unintuitive.

```
EmpEntities emp = new EmpEntities();

var query = from e in emp.Employees
            join d in emp.Departments
            on e.DeptID equals d.DeptID
            join w in emp.WorkLocations
            on e.EmployeeNum equals w.EmployNum
            join wl in emp.WorkLocationTypes
            on w.WorkTypeID equals wl.WorkLocationTypeID
            orderby e.LastName
            select new
            {
                e.FirstName, e.LastName,
                DepartmentName = d.Name,
                LocationName = w.Name,
                LocationType = wl.Name
            };

foreach (var a in query)
{
    Console.WriteLine(a.FirstName + " " + a.LastName +
                    " in " + a.DepartmentName +
                    " works at " + a.LocationName +
                    " which is " + a.LocationType);
}
```

Figure 79 - Multi-table JOIN with Query Syntax

While just the surface of Query Syntax has been covered there are two important items to note. First, the use of the `equals` keyword is required rather than the standard `==` operator. This is a requirement of the syntax and allows the compile to correctly identify table properties as opposed to simple comparable variables such as integer variables. Secondly the joins performed are all inner joins. Only the entities matched by the equal operator return in the result set. Outer joins are possible but require use of advanced LINQ which won't be covered in this book.

Finally, there is the ability to combine Fluent and Query syntax. One should keep in mind that Fluent methods are actually extension methods that mostly apply to collections. So one common use would be to "pre-process" the collection in the midst of a query. Examine the two queries in Figure 80 to see how each collection is processed using a Fluent method to restrict the members that are actually JOINed in the query.

While there is much, much more to LINQ the discussion presented up until now is a very good start. The basic selection and join syntax will most likely cover a very good range of data access needs. Additional LINQ-specific resources should be consulted for going further.

Also keep in mind that LINQ is about querying data; it is not used to change data. Manipulation of data is still done using object properties and the `SaveChanges()` method of the entities class. This implies that anonymous types aren't able to be saved. A data access strategy that encompasses a balance between presentation-only information and collections that are meant to be manipulated and persisted is important but beyond the scope of this book.

```
EmpEntities emp = new EmpEntities();
int top = 2;

// Only uses the top 2 salaries to join
var query =
    from e in emp.Employees.OrderBy(s =>s.Salary).Take(top)
    join d in emp.Departments
    on e.DeptID equals d.DeptID
    select new { e.LastName, d.Name };


// only joins with departments having more than 1 employee
var query2 =
    from e in emp.Employees
    join d in
    emp.Departments.Where( d => d.Employees.Count() >= top)
    on e.DeptID equals d.DeptID
    select new { e.LastName, d.Name };
```

Figure 80 - Combining Query and Fluent Syntax

Code First

Starting in Figure 56 a wizard was used to create an entity framework data model. This wizard examined an existing database and then created a set of entity and model classes based on those tables. It is possible to start with actual C# classes and have the framework create the database objects from those classes. This shields the developer from having to use any database tools.

This section will discuss the basics of Code First using a very simple example. Once the structure is complete querying and updating are the same as previously discussed.

The core of a Code First implementation is a concept known as the database context. In C# this is represented by the DbContext class and is derived from to create a project-specific context implementation. It also begins to illustrate that a principle known as "convention over configuration" is used quite extensively in Code First.

This type of context class has been seen before. In the EF model generated from a database in Figure 60, the EmpEntities class can be seen as being defined as a Context class. However this wasn't elaborated upon because it was a generated class and the focus was on the DbSet collections. In Code First this context-derived class is written manually and the backing database is created when the application is first run.

The code in Figure 81 shows a very basic class, ExampleContext, that derives from the framework DbContext class. It declares three public properties that are generic DbSet collections; these are the three tables in the database. Each table is defined in its own class and represents the table columns as properties. These are shown collectively in Figure 82.

Again, this is very similar to the code that was generated earlier from the wizard. However here the code is being hand-coded first. When the program is first run and the context class allocated the framework will detect that the database doesn't exist and will create the entire structure based on the class definitions. The resultant database structure is shown in Figure 84.

```
class ExampleContext : DbContext
{
    public DbSet<Employee> Employees { get; set; }
    public DbSet<Project> Projects { get; set; }
    public DbSet<ProjectDoc> ProjectDocs { get; set; }
}
```

Figure 81 - Simple Context class

Given only the code in Figures 81 and 82, how does the framework know what structures to create? This is where convention comes into play. Conventions can always be extended and overridden by the use of attributes but those options are so numerous only a few brief examples will be shown later in this section.

The first convention is actually the connection string for the ExampleContext class. The class shown in Figure 81 has no constructors defined, so the framework expects a connection string with the same name as the context defined in the application's configuration file. The setting in Figure 83 shows how this connection string looks. Note that additional constructors can be defined that take a connection string as an argument; this would allow for runtime specification of a connection string if needed.

Next is the convention for creating the table structures. The context defines three DbSet objects defining three tables based on the classes shown in Figure 82.

```csharp
public class Employee
{
    public Employee()
    {
        Projects = new List<Project>();
    }

    public Int32 EmployeeId { get; set; }
    public String FullName { get; set; }
    public DateTime BirthDate { get; set; }
    public Decimal Salary { get; set; }
    public String Title { get; set; }
    public virtual ICollection<Project> Projects
                                      { get; set; }
}

public class Project
{
    public Project ()
    {
        ProjectDocuments = new List<ProjectDoc>();
        Resources = new List<Employee>();
    }

    public Int32 ProjectId { get; set; }
    public String Name { get; set; }
    public DateTime Start { get; set; }
    public DateTime? End { get; set; }
    public virtual ICollection<ProjectDoc> ProjectDocuments
                                      { get; set; }
    public virtual ICollection<Employee> Resources
                                      { get; set; }
}

public class ProjectDoc
{
    public Int32 ProjectDocId { get; set; }
    public String DocName { get; set; }
    public String DocType { get; set; }
    public Project ReferringProject { get; set; }
}
```

Figure 82 - Entity Classes

```
<add name="ExampleContext"
    connectionString="Data Source=ec-pc\mssql_deved;
    Initial Catalog=SimpleCodeFirst;
    Integrated Security=True"
    providerName="System.Data.SqlClient" />
```

Figure 83 - ExampleContext Connection String

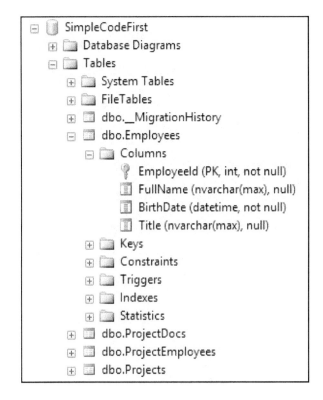

Figure 84 - Database from Code First

The name of each table will be the same as the class. Within each class the public properties will be implemented as columns in the tables. In addition if a column ends in "Id" it will be seen as the primary key of the table.

Entity Framework will map each C# type to a corresponding database type. Within types there are conventions that are applied. Some types are inherently nullable, such as `String`. This means that when translated to the database it will be defined as a `null` column meaning the value is not required. These defaults can sometimes be challenging as they can be different for different types. In the same class as `FullName` the `BirthDate` property is declared the same way yet it will be non-nullable.

Another convention is size and precision. By default the String type will be converted into a type of `nvarchar(max)` which is probably way more space than is needed. Decimal types also have a default mapping although none is shown here.

Attributes can be applied to the property values to override the default behavior. As stated above these can become very complex and the full range of possibilities will not be covered. However two simple attributes for strings.

For the String type, two common needs are to make it a non-nullable declaration and to control its length. This is accomplished using simple attributes. Figure 85 shows an updated declaration of the `FullName` property. This will result in the column being "`not null`" and "`nvarchar(100)`" when created in the database.

```
[MaxLength(100)]
[Required]
public String FullName { get; set; }
```

Figure 85 - Simple Column Attributes

The inverse way to turn a required type into a nullable
definition is by using the "?" operator on the property type
to make the type itself nullable. This will result in the
column also being nullable. The End property in the
Project class uses this convention to create a nullable SQL
column.

The convention to show relationships between objects is
with a member collection of the generic type
ICollection. This can represent both one-to-many and
many-to-many depending on where the collections are
defined. Each collection will be of the type that the
relationship. This is shown in Figure 82 in several places and
will be discussed further below.

The simplest is the Project class has a relationship to the
ProjectDoc class; a Project has a collection of related
ProjectDocs. In the ProjectDoc class there is a
reference back to a single Project. This is a simple one-
to-many relationship.

The second type of relationship is demonstrated between
the Employee and Project objects. An Employee can
have many Projects, and a Project can have many
Employees.

This is represented by a collection of related entities in each class. The framework will recognize this and create a Join table. This is shown in Figure 84 as the `ProjectEmployees` table and follows the same naming convention that was discussed earlier in the raw SQL section. The nice thing about Code First is that from a programmer perspective only objects and collections are accessed and multiple joins are handled by the framework.

A couple of notes about collections. The convention is to represent them as `public virtual ICollection<>`. The virtual modifier allows the framework to use lazy loading of the related collection as discussed earlier. If eager loading is need the virtual modifier can be left off. Also, the collection is initialized in the constructor with a concrete type (`new List()`). The actual concrete type of the collection obviously must implement the `ICollection` interface.

To use Code First to generate the database structure and subsequently manipulate data, code similar to the EF code shown previously is used. Figure 86 shows a section of code that instantiates an `ExampleContext` object and then manipulates objects from that. This was referred to as the "entities" object in the generated code; here the convention is to keep the name of "Context" to signify a context class. However this convention isn't required by any tooling or the framework in general. Manipulation of the objects themselves, including editing and saving, is the same as previously discussed.

```
try
{
    ExampleContext ec = new ExampleContext();

    List<Employee> e = ec.Employees.ToList();
    int EmpCount = e.Count;
    Console.WriteLine("There are " + EmpCount +
                      " employees right now");

    if ( EmpCount == 0)
    {
        Employee newEmp = new Employee
        {
            FullName = "Ted Test",
            BirthDate = new DateTime(1980, 04, 04),
            Salary = 100000,
            Title = "Web Developer"
        };

        e.Add(newEmp);
        ec.SaveChanges();

        Console.WriteLine("New employee added!");

    }
    else
    {
        foreach (Employee emp in e)
        {
            Console.WriteLine("Employee: " + emp.FullName);
        }
    }
}
catch (Exception ex)
{
    Console.WriteLine("Exception creating context: " +
                      ex.Message);
}
```

Figure 86 - Using Code First Classes

There are many entire books dedicated to Code First programming; this has been a very brief introduction that has barely scratched the surface. The structure here could easily be expanded out to many objects with many relations. There could also be very complex rules defined on columns and/or classes through the use of more complex attributes. However those are generally used in the same manner as the [Required] and [MaxLength] attributes above.

Also, as mentioned before, the connection string could be passed in when creating a context. This would be useful in situations where the connection string was environment dependent. Some organizations may have multiple environments such as Development, Integration Testing, User Testing, and Production. In these situations being able to determine which environment the code is in and use the appropriate connection string is essential.

Regardless of how the context/entity class is defined, using LINQ and objects to manipulate data can simplify programming. The developer only has to think in terms of objects rather than writing both C# code and SQL code. Of course that is still an option for difficult problems but using normal framework object manipulation should work most of the time.

Code First from a Database

In version 6.1 of Entity Framework Microsoft released another option for creating an EF Model. Code First from Database is a mix of the two previously discussed methods for generating a data model.

The main disadvantage with the "Database First" procedure was that the generated framework structure was not easily understood or editable at the code level. In Figure 60 the .edmx file is actually made up of .tt and .cs files and is not meant to be modified by programmers. However the model must be used when there is an existing database as is the case in many enterprise applications.

The main disadvantage to a "Code First" approach is that the database *cannot* exist before the first run of the application. And changes to the structure have to be run through the framework in a sometimes complicated migration structure. While this can actually be easy for small organizations where developers can where many hats and control their own databases, this is usually not the case in large organizations where separate distinct teams manage the databases.

Code First from Database strikes a good blend of the two methods to alleviate the two disadvantages described above. First, the database can exist such as for an existing application or in large enterprises. Second, the classes generated are based on DbContext and are based on the Code First style of simple classes and collections. The next several screenshots walk through the wizard steps when pointing to the Code First database created in the previous section.

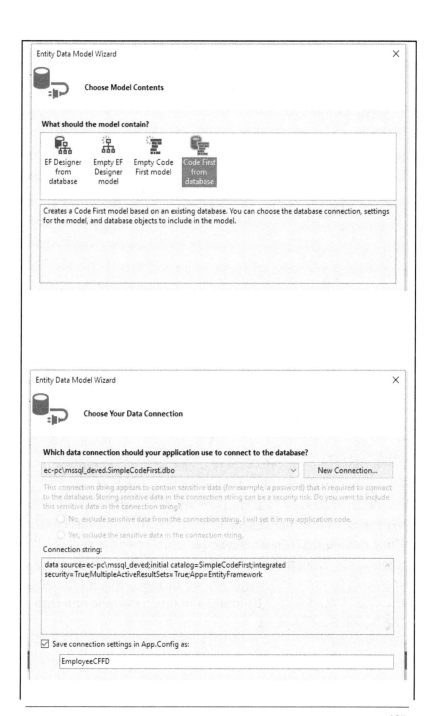

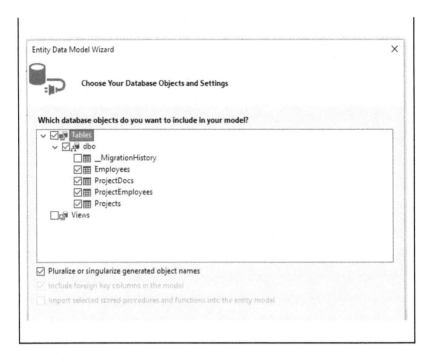

Figure 87 - Code First from Database Wizard Steps

Once the wizard has the tables specified it will complete the generation process. The steps were very similar to the previous "Database First" implementation with the exception of a few boxes being grayed out on the final step. Once the wizard finishes the code first classes are generated. The arrangement in the solution explorer is shown in Figure 88. This generated model is much simpler the first "Database First" model and much more in line with the "Code First" classes.

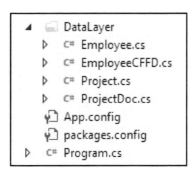

Figure 88 - Generated classes

One of the generated classes, Employee, is shown in Figure 89. This very similar to the hand-coded Code First. The exceptions are additional attributes, the class being declared partial, and the type of collection used.

The SuppressMessage attribute applied to the class and the reference collection are specific to suppressing warning messages from the compiler and certain code analysis tools. In both cases the implementation details of Code First violates warnings that can be ignored. The use of these attributes allows a clean compile.

The partial modifier for the class is a .NET construct that allows the definition of classes to span multiple files. This is also optional but allows for the clean separation of user code and wizard generated code. The wizard code could be removed and regenerated if the database changes while the user code would not change unless if references fields that change in the generated code. An example of common functionality to put in a user-defined file is in Figure 90. This would be in a separate folder but the name and namespace of the class are required to be the same.

```
public partial class Employee
{
    [System.Diagnostics.CodeAnalysis.SuppressMessage(
    "Microsoft.Usage",
    "CA2214:DoNotCallOverridableMethodsInConstructors")]
    public Employee()
    {
        Projects = new HashSet<Project>();
    }

    public int EmployeeId { get; set; }

    [Required]
    [StringLength(100)]
    public string FullName { get; set; }

    public DateTime BirthDate { get; set; }

    public string Title { get; set; }

    public decimal Salary { get; set; }

    [System.Diagnostics.CodeAnalysis.SuppressMessage(
    "Microsoft.Usage",
    "CA2227:CollectionPropertiesShouldBeReadOnly")]
    public virtual ICollection<Project> Projects
                                        { get; set; }
}
```

Figure 89 - Generated Employee Code

```
public partial class Employee
{
    public override String ToString()
    {
        return this.FullName + "(" + this.EmployeeId + ")";
    }
}
```

Figure 90 - User Function in Partial Class

Finally, the generated code uses a `HashSet` rather than the handcoded `List` for the reference collection. Both implement the `ICollection` interface and are acceptable to use. However the `HashSet` doesn't allow duplicate objects. Depending on how important it is to enforce this limitation in code is up to the programmer as the database also enforces this with primary keys.

Programming Summary

The methods described in this section are a good introduction to database programming with C#. From ADO.NET and DataSets through to Entity Framework with LINQ the reader should be able to understand more complex code in an existing project, or create a new system using the techniques shown here. Although this has been a basic introduction the concepts are easy to extend. And as can been in the last Code First From Database example simple classes are becoming more standard with the Framework taking care of much of the boilerplate code, some of which could be complex and error prone if manually written.

It also should be noted that even though all the previous examples were in .NET/C#, many other frameworks have similar concepts and practices. Java has many ORM frameworks, one of the more popular being Hibernate. Although the syntax is slightly different than EF the use of classes to represent tables and programming again those classes in the framework is very similar. The reader shouldn't have too much of a problem to make a cross-language leap either.

Summary

This book has discussed and demonstrated the basics of database design, SQL programming, and programming using different forms of data frameworks. The intent of this short introduction is to begin the process of learning. The principles and examples herein could be successful on small projects with not much in the way of scaling. Many simple websites and applications can have less than a dozen tables and everything discussed in here would suit that type of application well.

However larger enterprise applications may have several dozens of tables capturing and relating much more layers of information. These applications may also make use of advanced programming techniques such as stored procedures, triggers, and complex cascading-delete schemes. None of those were discussed here but the reader is encouraged to travel further into these advanced topics after completing this book.

The reader is also encouraged to expand on the data frameworks section. Not only are there other ORM mechanisms out there, there are also many query languages supporting many types of data. Because of the proliferation of SQL many are based on the "select/from/where" ideas.

Finally, No-SQL databases are also popular these days. These storage engines store objects in a non-relational way that may be optimized for space or retrieval speed. However many of these also have a SQL-like query interface to ease the transition from relational to non-relational data.

Clearly SQL and SQL programming are an important tool in the programmers toolbox.

Bibliography

Codd, E. F. (2000). *The Relational Model for Database Management: Version 2.* Reading, MA. Addison Wesley

Albahari, Joseph and Ben (2016) *C# Pocket Reference.* Sebastopol, CA O'Reilly

Appendix

Full Script for creating and populating a sample database. Many of the statements were generated by SQL Management Studio after creating the objects via the GUI. Many of the "ALTER" statements are a method for setting database options that are visually done with a checkbox, dropdown, etc.

These scripts are meant to be run a GUI editor such as SQL Management Studio. If the path to the datafile is different or any other options need to be changed they should be changed before running the scripts.

These scripts actually exist in separate files. The name of each file is given in bold before each set of statements.

CreateDatabaseStatements.sql

```
USE [master]
GO

/* Create the database */
/* This statement assumes the path C:\Projects\DATA exists. */

CREATE DATABASE [JustEnoughEmployee]
 CONTAINMENT = NONE
 ON  PRIMARY
( NAME = N'JustEnoughEmployee', FILENAME =
N'C:\Projects\DATA\JustEnoughEmployee.mdf' , SIZE = 4096KB ,
MAXSIZE = UNLIMITED, FILEGROWTH = 1024KB )
 LOG ON
( NAME = N'JustEnoughEmployee_log', FILENAME =
N'C:\Projects\DATA\JustEnoughEmployee_log.ldf' , SIZE = 2048KB ,
MAXSIZE = 2048GB , FILEGROWTH = 10%)
```

```
GO

/* Set some common properties */

ALTER DATABASE [JustEnoughEmployee] SET COMPATIBILITY_LEVEL =
110
GO

IF (1 = FULLTEXTSERVICEPROPERTY('IsFullTextInstalled'))
begin
EXEC [JustEnoughEmployee].[dbo].[sp_fulltext_database] @action =
'enable'
end
GO

ALTER DATABASE [JustEnoughEmployee] SET ANSI_NULL_DEFAULT OFF
GO

ALTER DATABASE [JustEnoughEmployee] SET ANSI_NULLS OFF
GO

ALTER DATABASE [JustEnoughEmployee] SET ANSI_PADDING OFF
GO

ALTER DATABASE [JustEnoughEmployee] SET ANSI_WARNINGS OFF
GO

ALTER DATABASE [JustEnoughEmployee] SET ARITHABORT OFF
GO

ALTER DATABASE [JustEnoughEmployee] SET AUTO_CLOSE OFF
GO

ALTER DATABASE [JustEnoughEmployee] SET AUTO_CREATE_STATISTICS
ON
GO

ALTER DATABASE [JustEnoughEmployee] SET AUTO_SHRINK OFF
GO
```

```
ALTER DATABASE [JustEnoughEmployee] SET AUTO_UPDATE_STATISTICS
ON
GO

ALTER DATABASE [JustEnoughEmployee] SET
CURSOR_CLOSE_ON_COMMIT OFF
GO

ALTER DATABASE [JustEnoughEmployee] SET CURSOR_DEFAULT
GLOBAL
GO

ALTER DATABASE [JustEnoughEmployee] SET
CONCAT_NULL_YIELDS_NULL OFF
GO

ALTER DATABASE [JustEnoughEmployee] SET NUMERIC_ROUNDABORT
OFF
GO

ALTER DATABASE [JustEnoughEmployee] SET QUOTED_IDENTIFIER OFF
GO

ALTER DATABASE [JustEnoughEmployee] SET RECURSIVE_TRIGGERS OFF
GO

ALTER DATABASE [JustEnoughEmployee] SET  DISABLE_BROKER
GO

ALTER DATABASE [JustEnoughEmployee] SET
AUTO_UPDATE_STATISTICS_ASYNC OFF
GO

ALTER DATABASE [JustEnoughEmployee] SET
DATE_CORRELATION_OPTIMIZATION OFF
GO

ALTER DATABASE [JustEnoughEmployee] SET TRUSTWORTHY OFF
GO
```

```
ALTER DATABASE [JustEnoughEmployee] SET
ALLOW_SNAPSHOT_ISOLATION OFF
GO

ALTER DATABASE [JustEnoughEmployee] SET PARAMETERIZATION
SIMPLE
GO

ALTER DATABASE [JustEnoughEmployee] SET
READ_COMMITTED_SNAPSHOT OFF
GO

ALTER DATABASE [JustEnoughEmployee] SET HONOR_BROKER_PRIORITY
OFF
GO

ALTER DATABASE [JustEnoughEmployee] SET RECOVERY FULL
GO

ALTER DATABASE [JustEnoughEmployee] SET  MULTI_USER
GO

ALTER DATABASE [JustEnoughEmployee] SET PAGE_VERIFY CHECKSUM
GO

ALTER DATABASE [JustEnoughEmployee] SET DB_CHAINING OFF
GO

ALTER DATABASE [JustEnoughEmployee] SET FILESTREAM(
NON_TRANSACTED_ACCESS = OFF )
GO

ALTER DATABASE [JustEnoughEmployee] SET TARGET_RECOVERY_TIME
= 0 SECONDS
GO

ALTER DATABASE [JustEnoughEmployee] SET  READ_WRITE
GO
```

CreateEmployeeTable.sql

```
USE [JustEnoughEmployee]
GO

SET ANSI_NULLS ON
GO

SET QUOTED_IDENTIFIER ON
GO

SET ANSI_PADDING ON
GO

CREATE TABLE [dbo].[Employee](
        [EmployeeNum] [int] NOT NULL,
        [LastName] [varchar](50) NOT NULL,
        [FirstName] [varchar](30) NOT NULL,
        [HomeAddress] [varchar](50) NOT NULL,
        [Salary] [money] NOT NULL,
        [FullTime] [bit] NOT NULL,
        [DeptID] [int] NULL,
 CONSTRAINT [PK_Employee] PRIMARY KEY CLUSTERED
(
        [EmployeeNum] ASC
)WITH (PAD_INDEX = OFF, STATISTICS_NORECOMPUTE = OFF,
IGNORE_DUP_KEY = OFF, ALLOW_ROW_LOCKS = ON,
ALLOW_PAGE_LOCKS = ON) ON [PRIMARY]
) ON [PRIMARY]

GO

SET ANSI_PADDING OFF
GO

-- NOTE: This may have to be run AFTER the Department table is created.
ALTER TABLE [dbo].[Employee]  WITH CHECK ADD  CONSTRAINT
[FK_Employee_Department] FOREIGN KEY([DeptID])
REFERENCES [dbo].[Department] ([DeptID])
GO
```

```
ALTER TABLE [dbo].[Employee] CHECK CONSTRAINT
[FK_Employee_Department]
GO
```

CreateDepartmentTable.sql

```
USE [JustEnoughEmployee]
GO

SET ANSI_NULLS ON
GO

SET QUOTED_IDENTIFIER ON
GO

SET ANSI_PADDING ON
GO

CREATE TABLE [dbo].[Department](
        [DeptID] [int] IDENTITY(1,1) NOT NULL,
        [Name] [varchar](50) NOT NULL,
        [IsTechnical] [char](1) NOT NULL,
        [ManagerID] [int] NULL,
 CONSTRAINT [PK_Department] PRIMARY KEY CLUSTERED
(
        [DeptID] ASC
)WITH (PAD_INDEX = OFF, STATISTICS_NORECOMPUTE = OFF,
IGNORE_DUP_KEY = OFF, ALLOW_ROW_LOCKS = ON,
ALLOW_PAGE_LOCKS = ON) ON [PRIMARY]
) ON [PRIMARY]

GO

SET ANSI_PADDING OFF
GO

ALTER TABLE [dbo].[Department]  WITH CHECK ADD  CONSTRAINT
[FK_Department_Employee] FOREIGN KEY([ManagerID])
```

REFERENCES [dbo].[Employee] ([EmployeeNum])
GO

ALTER TABLE [dbo].[Department] CHECK CONSTRAINT
[FK_Department_Employee]
GO

CREATE UNIQUE NONCLUSTERED INDEX IX_MANAGERID_NOTNULL
ON Department(ManagerID)
WHERE ManagerID IS NOT NULL;

CreateProjectTable.sql

```
USE [JustEnoughEmployee]
GO

SET ANSI_NULLS ON
GO

SET QUOTED_IDENTIFIER ON
GO

SET ANSI_PADDING ON
GO

CREATE TABLE [dbo].[Project](
        [ProjectID] [int] IDENTITY(1,1) NOT NULL,
        [ProjectName] [varchar](30) NOT NULL,
        [StartDate] [date] NOT NULL,
        [PercentComplete] [int] NOT NULL,
        [Summary] [varchar](200) NULL,
        [DepartmentID] [int] NULL,
 CONSTRAINT [PK_Project] PRIMARY KEY CLUSTERED
(
        [ProjectID] ASC
)WITH (PAD_INDEX = OFF, STATISTICS_NORECOMPUTE = OFF,
IGNORE_DUP_KEY = OFF, ALLOW_ROW_LOCKS = ON,
ALLOW_PAGE_LOCKS = ON) ON [PRIMARY]
) ON [PRIMARY]
```

```
GO

SET ANSI_PADDING OFF
GO

ALTER TABLE [dbo].[Project] ADD  CONSTRAINT
[DF_Project_PercentComplete]  DEFAULT ((0)) FOR [PercentComplete]
GO

ALTER TABLE [dbo].[Project] WITH CHECK ADD  CONSTRAINT
[FK_Project_Department] FOREIGN KEY([DepartmentID])
REFERENCES [dbo].[Department] ([DeptID])
GO

ALTER TABLE [dbo].[Project] CHECK CONSTRAINT
[FK_Project_Department]
GO
```

CreateEmployeeProjectTable.sql

```
USE [JustEnoughEmployee]
GO

SET ANSI_NULLS ON
GO

SET QUOTED_IDENTIFIER ON
GO

CREATE TABLE [dbo].[EmployeeProject](
        [EmployNum] [int] NOT NULL,
        [ProjectID] [int] NOT NULL,
 CONSTRAINT [PK_EmployeeProject] PRIMARY KEY CLUSTERED
(
        [EmployNum] ASC,
        [ProjectID] ASC
```

```
)WITH (PAD_INDEX = OFF, STATISTICS_NORECOMPUTE = OFF,
IGNORE_DUP_KEY = OFF, ALLOW_ROW_LOCKS = ON,
ALLOW_PAGE_LOCKS = ON) ON [PRIMARY]
) ON [PRIMARY]

GO

ALTER TABLE [dbo].[EmployeeProject] WITH CHECK ADD  CONSTRAINT
[FK_EmployeeProject_Employee] FOREIGN KEY([EmployNum])
REFERENCES [dbo].[Employee] ([EmployeeNum])
GO

ALTER TABLE [dbo].[EmployeeProject] CHECK CONSTRAINT
[FK_EmployeeProject_Employee]
GO

ALTER TABLE [dbo].[EmployeeProject] WITH CHECK ADD  CONSTRAINT
[FK_EmployeeProject_Project] FOREIGN KEY([ProjectID])
REFERENCES [dbo].[Project] ([ProjectID])
GO

ALTER TABLE [dbo].[EmployeeProject] CHECK CONSTRAINT
[FK_EmployeeProject_Project]
GO
```

CreateWorkLocationType.sql

```
USE [JustEnoughEmployee]
GO

SET ANSI_NULLS ON
GO

SET QUOTED_IDENTIFIER ON
GO

SET ANSI_PADDING ON
GO

CREATE TABLE [dbo].[WorkLocationType](
```

```sql
	[WorkLocationTypeID] [int] IDENTITY(1,1) NOT NULL,
	[Name] [varchar](20) NOT NULL,
	[Description] [varchar](50) NULL,
 CONSTRAINT [PK_WorkLocationType] PRIMARY KEY CLUSTERED
(
	[WorkLocationTypeID] ASC
)WITH (PAD_INDEX = OFF, STATISTICS_NORECOMPUTE = OFF,
IGNORE_DUP_KEY = OFF, ALLOW_ROW_LOCKS = ON,
ALLOW_PAGE_LOCKS = ON) ON [PRIMARY]
) ON [PRIMARY]

GO

SET ANSI_PADDING OFF
GO
```

CreateWorkLocation.sql

```sql
USE [JustEnoughEmployee]
GO

SET ANSI_NULLS ON
GO

SET QUOTED_IDENTIFIER ON
GO

SET ANSI_PADDING ON
GO

CREATE TABLE [dbo].[WorkLocation](
	[WorkLocationID] [int] IDENTITY(1,1) NOT NULL,
	[Name] [varchar](30) NOT NULL,
	[Description] [varchar](50) NULL,
	[EmployNum] [int] NULL,
	[WorkTypeID] [int] NOT NULL,
 CONSTRAINT [PK_WorkLocation] PRIMARY KEY CLUSTERED
(
	[WorkLocationID] ASC
```

```sql
)WITH (PAD_INDEX = OFF, STATISTICS_NORECOMPUTE = OFF,
IGNORE_DUP_KEY = OFF, ALLOW_ROW_LOCKS = ON,
ALLOW_PAGE_LOCKS = ON) ON [PRIMARY]
) ON [PRIMARY]

GO

SET ANSI_PADDING OFF
GO

ALTER TABLE [dbo].[WorkLocation]  WITH CHECK ADD  CONSTRAINT
[FK_WorkLocation_Employee] FOREIGN KEY([EmployNum])
REFERENCES [dbo].[Employee] ([EmployeeNum])
GO

ALTER TABLE [dbo].[WorkLocation] CHECK CONSTRAINT
[FK_WorkLocation_Employee]
GO

ALTER TABLE [dbo].[WorkLocation]  WITH CHECK ADD  CONSTRAINT
[FK_WorkLocation_WorkLocationType] FOREIGN KEY([WorkTypeID])
REFERENCES [dbo].[WorkLocationType] ([WorkLocationTypeID])
GO

ALTER TABLE [dbo].[WorkLocation] CHECK CONSTRAINT
[FK_WorkLocation_WorkLocationType]
GO
```

DataInsert.sql

```sql
/*
Populate data in the database
*/

/* Employees */

INSERT INTO Employee (EmployeeNum, Lastname, FirstName,
        HomeAddress, Salary, FullTime)
VALUES (22, 'Johnson', 'Ted', '123 Ted Street',
                100000.00, 1)
```

```
INSERT INTO Employee (EmployeeNum, Lastname, FirstName,
    HomeAddress, Salary, FullTime)
VALUES (33, 'Wexley', 'Joann', '454 CID Place',
    110000.00, 1)

INSERT INTO Employee (EmployeeNum, Lastname, FirstName,
    HomeAddress, Salary, FullTime)
VALUES (44, 'Wonderland', 'Alice', 'The Yellowbrick Road',
    97000.00, 1)

INSERT INTO Employee (EmployeeNum, Lastname, FirstName,
    HomeAddress, Salary, FullTime)
VALUES (55, 'Daboss', 'Tom', '1 King Street',
    150000.00, 1)

INSERT INTO Employee (EmployeeNum, Lastname, FirstName,
    HomeAddress, Salary, FullTime)
VALUES (66, 'Moore', 'Gary', '6 String Blvd',
    115000.00, 1)

INSERT INTO Employee (EmployeeNum, Lastname, FirstName,
    HomeAddress, Salary, FullTime)
VALUES (77, 'Sister', 'Twisted', 'Take It Lane',
    107000.00, 1)

INSERT INTO Employee (EmployeeNum, Lastname, FirstName,
    HomeAddress, Salary, FullTime)
VALUES (88, 'Wilde', 'Zack', '88 Big Band Street',
    121000.00, 1)


/* Department */
INSERT INTO Department (Name, IsTechnical)
VALUES ('External Programming', 1)

INSERT INTO Department (Name, IsTechnical)
VALUES ('Internal Programming', 1)

INSERT INTO Department (Name, IsTechnical)
```

```sql
VALUES ('Marketing', 0)

INSERT INTO Department (Name, IsTechnical)
VALUES ('HR', 0)

INSERT INTO Department (Name, IsTechnical)
VALUES ('Infrastructure', 1)


/* Work Loc Type */
INSERT INTO WorkLocationType (Name,[Description])
VALUES ('Office', 'Primary office building')

INSERT INTO WorkLocationType (Name,[Description])
VALUES ('Home', 'Employee home office')

INSERT INTO WorkLocationType (Name,[Description])
VALUES ('Shared', 'Shared office space')

/* Work Location */
INSERT INTO WorkLocation (Name, [Description],
        EmployNum, WorkTypeID)
VALUES ('Room 1', 'Office Number 1',
22,
(SELECT WorkLocationTypeID from WorkLocationType
WHERE Name = 'Office') )


INSERT INTO WorkLocation (Name, [Description],
        EmployNum, WorkTypeID)
VALUES ('Room 2', 'Office Number 2',
33,
(SELECT WorkLocationTypeID from WorkLocationType
WHERE Name = 'Office') )

INSERT INTO WorkLocation (Name, [Description],
        EmployNum, WorkTypeID)
VALUES ('Room 3', 'Office Number 3',
44,
(SELECT WorkLocationTypeID from WorkLocationType
```

```
WHERE Name = 'Office') )

INSERT INTO WorkLocation (Name, [Description],
        EmployNum, WorkTypeID)
VALUES ('Room 4', 'Office Number 4',
55,
(SELECT WorkLocationTypeID from WorkLocationType
WHERE Name = 'Office') )

INSERT INTO WorkLocation (Name, [Description],
        EmployNum, WorkTypeID)
VALUES ('Room 5', 'Office Number 5',
55,
(SELECT WorkLocationTypeID from WorkLocationType
WHERE Name = 'Office') )

INSERT INTO WorkLocation (Name, [Description],
        EmployNum, WorkTypeID)
VALUES ('Home Office', 'Personal home office',
66,
(SELECT WorkLocationTypeID from WorkLocationType
WHERE Name = 'Home') )


/* Project */

INSERT INTO Project (ProjectName, StartDate,
                PercentComplete, Summary, DepartmentID)
VALUES('Xamarin Mobile App', '3-JUL-2017',
            0, 'Simple Xamarin POC for HR',
            (SELECT DeptID FROM Department WHERE
NAME='HR'))

INSERT INTO Project (ProjectName, StartDate,
                PercentComplete, Summary, DepartmentID)
VALUES('Benefits Cost Summary', '6-Feb-2017',
            65, 'Calculate Employee Benefits cost',
            (SELECT DeptID FROM Department WHERE
NAME='HR'))
```

```
INSERT INTO Project (ProjectName, StartDate,
                      PercentComplete, Summary)
VALUES('Package Manager Summary Site', '12-Dec-2016',
        90, 'Lists approved development packages',
        (SELECT DeptID FROM Department
         WHERE NAME='Internal Programming'))

INSERT INTO Project (ProjectName, StartDate,
                      PercentComplete, Summary, DepartmentID)
VALUES('Lead Follow-up tracker', '4-Mar-2017',
        0, 'Leads for Marketing',
        (SELECT DeptID FROM Department
         WHERE NAME='Marketing'))

/* Employee Project */
INSERT INTO EmployeeProject (EmployNum, ProjectID)
VALUES(
(SELECT EmployeeNum from Employee Where LastName='Johnson'),
(SELECT ProjectID from Project where ProjectName LIKE 'Xamarin%') )

INSERT INTO EmployeeProject (EmployNum, ProjectID)
VALUES(
(SELECT EmployeeNum from Employee Where LastName='Wexley'),
(SELECT ProjectID from Project where ProjectName LIKE 'Xamarin%') )

INSERT INTO EmployeeProject (EmployNum, ProjectID)
VALUES(
(SELECT EmployeeNum from Employee Where
LastName='Wonderland'),
(SELECT ProjectID from Project where ProjectName LIKE 'Xamarin%') )

INSERT INTO EmployeeProject (EmployNum, ProjectID)
VALUES(
(SELECT EmployeeNum from Employee Where LastName='Johnson'),
(SELECT ProjectID from Project where ProjectName LIKE 'Benefits%') )

INSERT INTO EmployeeProject (EmployNum, ProjectID)
VALUES(
```

```
(SELECT EmployeeNum from Employee Where
LastName='Wonderland'),
(SELECT ProjectID from Project where ProjectName LIKE 'Benefits%') )

INSERT INTO EmployeeProject (EmployNum, ProjectID)
VALUES(
(SELECT EmployeeNum from Employee Where LastName='Daboss'),
(SELECT ProjectID from Project where ProjectName LIKE 'Xamarin%') )

INSERT INTO EmployeeProject (EmployNum, ProjectID)
VALUES(
(SELECT EmployeeNum from Employee Where LastName='Wilde'),
(SELECT ProjectID from Project where ProjectName LIKE 'Package%') )

INSERT INTO EmployeeProject (EmployNum, ProjectID)
VALUES(
(SELECT EmployeeNum from Employee Where LastName='Wilde'),
(SELECT ProjectID from Project where ProjectName LIKE 'Lead%') )

INSERT INTO EmployeeProject (EmployNum, ProjectID)
VALUES(
(SELECT EmployeeNum from Employee Where LastName='Sister'),
(SELECT ProjectID from Project where ProjectName LIKE 'Lead%') )

INSERT INTO EmployeeProject (EmployNum, ProjectID)
VALUES(
(SELECT EmployeeNum from Employee Where LastName='Moore'),
(SELECT ProjectID from Project where ProjectName LIKE 'Lead%') )
```

www.ingramcontent.com/pod-product-compliance
Lightning Source LLC
LaVergne TN
LVHW022322060326
832902LV00020B/3618